Foreign Travelers in America
1810–1935

Foreign Travelers in America
1810–1935

Advisory Editors:

Arthur M. Schlesinger, Jr.
Eugene P. Moehring

My American Visit

Frederick [Edwin] Smith

(Lord Birkenhead)

ARNO PRESS
A New York Times Company
New York—1974

Reprint Edition 1974 by Arno Press Inc.

Copyright © 1918 by Hutchinson & Co.
Reprinted by permission of Hutchinson
  Publishing Group Ltd.

Reprinted from a copy in the State Historical
  Society of Wisconsin Library

FOREIGN TRAVELERS IN AMERICA, 1810-1935
ISBN for complete set: 0-405-05440-8
See last pages of this volume for titles.

Manufactured in the United States of America

Library of Congress Cataloging in Publication Data

Birkenhead, Frederick Edwin Smith, 1st Earl of,
    1872-1930.
    My American visit.

    (Foreign travelers in America, 1810-1935)
    Reprint of the ed. published by Hutchinson, London.
    1. European War, 1914-1918--United States.
2. United States--Description and travel--1900-1920.
3. European War, 1914-1918--Canada. I. Title.
II. Series.
D619.B55 1974   917.3'04'913   73-13150
ISBN 0-405-05473-4

My American Visit

PRESIDENT WILSON:
"The challenge is to
all mankind.
The wrongs against
which we now array
ourselves cut to the
very root of human life

[Frontispiece.

My American Visit

By The Rt. Hon. Sir Frederick Smith, Bart., *His Majesty's Attorney-General, Treasurer of Gray's Inn, Hon. Fellow of Wadham College, Oxford* :: :: :: ::

LONDON: HUTCHINSON & CO.
PATERNOSTER ROW :: :: 1918

TO THE PEOPLE

OF THE

UNITED STATES

AND

TO MY FELLOW CITIZENS IN THE
DOMINION OF CANADA

IN SLIGHT ACKNOWLEDGMENT OF GREAT KINDNESSES
RECEIVED IN BOTH COUNTRIES
I DEDICATE THIS BRIEF RECORD OF MY TRAVELS

F. E. S.

"In God's name, cheerily on, courageous friends,
To reap the harvest of perpetual peace,
By this one bloody trial of sharp war."
                                        Shakspeare.
                                        " *Richard III.*'

"Waterloo did more than any other battle I know of
towards the true object of all battles—the peace of the
world."—*The Duke of Wellington.*

PREFACE

I HAD arranged to spend Christmas with my family at Blenheim, when quite unexpectedly I was asked by Sir Edward Carson, on behalf of the War Cabinet, whether it would be possible for me, having regard to my legal engagements, to go to the United States for six weeks or two months. This invitation was strongly supported by Lord Northcliffe, and my old friend, Lord Reading, whom I naturally consulted, took the same view. I had in my own department many matters which required discussion with Washington, but apart from this, it was thought desirable that some British Minister should at this moment visit the United States and Canada, and, for reasons into which it is not necessary to enter, it was not possible for others to go. I saw the Prime Minister in his room at the House of Commons on the 15th December, only two days after Sir Edward Carson first made the proposal to me, and it was settled there and then.

I was allowed two private secretaries, Colonel M. and H. S. The correspondence with which I was confronted throughout the tour would have kept six secretaries occupied, and my acknowledgments to them for faithful and most friendly service may be rendered here once for all. Their diaries are indeed the foundation of this narrative. They have corrected what I have dictated, and have supplemented my memory in almost every page.

I ought to add that there were three additional reasons which made it convenient, if possible, that I should undertake this journey. There were various legal matters, long the subject of correspondence between myself and various American colleagues, which could be more conveniently adjusted by discussion. I had been invited with Colonel Roosevelt to give the annual address at the Ohio Banquet in New York. Almost by the same post arrived a pressing invitation to deliver the annual address to the New York Bar Association. And so it came about that we left Euston at 5.30 p.m. on Monday, the 17th of December. The only other member of the party was Troubridge, my servant, who, so far as any member of the party observed, never smiled from the moment he left Liverpool, but still rendered patient service amid surroundings which he was never able to understand.

I have been, and still am, in great doubt as to whether these random records of so hurried a tour* will interest anyone. I cannot possibly, having regard to my engagements when I reach London, attempt to present them in any very readable form. But I have, on the whole, decided to use

---

* Paget, M.P., was, in comparison, a pottering dawdler.

Col. M.   F. E. S.   and   H. S.

[To face p. vi.

the monotonous days of a long voyage under convoy to preserve some record of the diaries one or the other of us has kept.

Many considerations led me to this view. No one need read this casual and informal record who does not wish to, and certainly no one is compelled to buy it, but the part played by America in this war must be a decisive part, if any decision at all is to be reached. Our tour in America took place at a very critical stage in the preparations of America. We had opportunities of making the acquaintance of, and of talking frankly with, many of the leading men in America. We travelled in two months nearly fifteen thousand miles, from Liverpool to Liverpool. I addressed in that period forty-eight meetings, generally three and once five a day. In the aggregate, I spoke, on a careful computation, to 100,000 people. Many of these audiences were very representative, consisting of Bar Associations and Chambers of Commerce. These meetings usually took place in the day time and were followed by mass meetings in the evenings, often consisting of five or six thousand people. It may therefore be reasonably claimed that I had very unusual opportunities of becoming acquainted with the present attitude of the people of America. However casual and blurred my impressions, I am not without the hope that they may be of interest to my countrymen.

It seemed to me that I was fortunate in the opportunity of visiting the States at this supremely

interesting moment. America cannot win the
war without us, and we cannot win the war
without America. The views of the two countries upon all the principal issues seem to me
to be identical. Both are agreed that a Germany
which emerged from the war triumphant in the
East, and with immensely increased territories as
the reward of International outrage, would throw
the whole world into permanent armed camps.
In such a contingency we need not trouble about
the League of Nations. No concessions to France or
Belgium can alter this circumstance. Germany
has defied the conscience of mankind and torn up
the Public Law of the World. She either succeeds
or she fails. No half-way house is conceivable.

These facts are, I think, realized in England.
They are certainly very clearly realized in the States.
No better statement of the mental process through
which Americans have passed could be desired than
that recently made by Mr. Gompers, the President
of the American Federation of Labour :

" I lived in a fool's paradise," he said, " I have
believed in men ; believed that, when they solemnly
pledged themselves and those in whose name they
were authorized to speak, they would go to the
limit in their own countries to prevent the rupture
of international peace. I believed them, for I
felt that I would have gone to the furthest limit
to uphold those pledges. Almost out of a clear sky
came the declaration of war, and I found the men
who pledged their word to me and mine to maintain

peace, flying to the colours of the greatest autocrat
of all time—a scientific, intellectual murderer—
flying to attack their brothers whose lives they
pledged themselves to protect; and from then
until the peace of the world is assured I count
myself transformed from a pacifist into a living,
breathing fighting man."

This attitude is, in my judgment, typical of the
whole nation, and the narrative, however superficial,
of a visit to such a nation, at such a moment,
cannot altogether fail in interest.

But I have a more intimate reason for preserving
some record of a very remarkable tour. We have
never in our lives received so much kindness, so
much friendship, and, in many cases, I may add,
so much affection, from those who were strangers
to us when we landed in New York. However
feeble my expression of gratitude may be, I am
determined to make it. Many people on a superficial acquaintance have formed the view that the
American nation is hard, practical, material and
unsentimental. It may be that this impression
is the result of an unconscious national pose in
the States. I have now quite clearly formed the
view, having some acquaintance with foreign nations,
that no country in the world is warmer-hearted,
more generous, more sentimental and, above all,
more tolerant of rhetoric than America. I would
almost venture to apply to them the language
in which Tacitus described an earlier generation :
" *Facile perferebat ille populus impeditissimarum*

*orationum spatia, atque id ipsum laudabat si dicendo
quis diem eximeret.''** But it must be understood
that I have in my mind not their attitude to their
own excellent speakers, but the indulgence with
which they supported my over-driven hack.

If this war yields nothing else that is good, it
will certainly end once for all the misunderstandings
between Great Britain and the United States.
Those misunderstandings, partly the result of bad
statesmanship, partly of mutual ignorance, partly
of superficial social differences, have enjoyed a
vitality as surprising as it has been mischievous. It
cannot and will not survive the comradeship of this
war. I am bewildered when I recall, or try to recall,
the thousands of friendly hands which I have grasped
during my visit. To all those who have been kind
to us I offer, in this brief record, an unworthy
expression of my thanks. If it helps in any
degree, however small, to make my countrymen
understand what the real American thinks of
England to-day, I shall be content. And if I fail,
I lose nothing but the long days of a voyage in
which there is little useful competitive occupation.

And I desire here, with all the earnestness at my
command, and with the experience which it will be
conceded that I possess, to insist upon the importance of sending British speakers to the United
States and American speakers to Great Britain.
It was a poignant but pregnant question which

* They much preferred the longest possible speeches, and
delighted in him who would fill up the day with rhetoric

a great French caricaturist imagined one poilu
putting to another in the trenches : " *Mon brave,
tu crois que les civiles tiendront ?* " It has now,
far too late, become a commonplace of the war that
the morale of the civilians is as vital, to its effective
prosecution, as the morale of the soldiers. Those
who attempt to drive a wedge between the politicians and the soldiers in our own country, or in any
Allied country, are, in fact, whether they know it or
not, playing the game of the enemy. Both the
politicians and the soldiers are essential to one
another. If the politicians fail, as they failed in
Russia, to do their part of the work, and control
their share of the national fortunes, the soldiers are
the first to suffer. The collapse of the political
machine, in that unhappy country, was made red
with the blood of admirals and generals.

For this reason, those of the Allies who speak
the same language, are greatly culpable if they
neglect any opportunity of getting into closer touch
with one another.

Competent English speakers, with the gift of
forcible and direct expression, ought, therefore,
to visit the States to remind Americans of what we
have done and what we are still resolute to do.

And let American speakers, with powers of speech
which will enable them to command large audiences,
come to England and tell those in our midst, who are
war-weary, what I have tried in this volume to tell
them, that if they hold their line just a little longer,
the intervention of the United States will secure

for them all the fruits of their long and bitter
sacrifice.

It will be observed that the pages which follow
are not without reference to occasions of recreation,
and even of gaiety, in the United States. I have
been very careful to lay stress upon this branch of
our observation. " A man who is at home in the
world laughs and is gay," writes Price Collier in
his " Germany and the Germans." And the saying
is as true of war as it is true of peace. Perhaps
even truer, for human nature, when intolerably
racked, claims, ever more and more imperiously,
the recreations of a lighter atmosphere. The
victims of the Guillotine danced to the very moment
when the Door of Death opened. The theatres
played to full audiences almost all through the
Siege of Paris. The tragedies of our own Civil
War were followed by the license of the Restoration.
Sing-songs are an institution in France. The
soldier in the trenches—officer and private—dreams
not of a drab and pleasureless Blighty, but of one
which provides him with his own particular concep-
tions of social enjoyment.

And in any event it is my purpose to describe
America as I saw it, and as I understood it.
Such a picture, if truthful, must make it plain
that the United States, like Great Britain, and like
suffering France, is not prepared to immolate the
spirit of social gaiety, and the relaxations of pleasure, even in face of the Moloch of this war.

A special word should, perhaps, be said about the

Canadian part of the tour. No Englishman can think, much less speak, without emotion of the part which Canada has played in this war. I delight to place on record for the encouragement of those—if any such there be—in England who falter in their task, the great message of spiritual inspiration which is almost the greatest of Canada's contributions to this war. Everywhere in Canada one meets war widows, orphans, bereaved parents. They have lost all they loved in remote battlefields. It is only obvious to the more thoughtful among them how direct is the interest of Canada in the war. And yet their spirit is as high after three and a half years as it was in August, 1914. They have carried conscription in the face of difficulties, which we at least have every reason to understand, and they send to the Mother Country to-day a message of unconquerable resolution.

I ought to add that I was profoundly struck by the generous admiration felt and expressed in the United States for the valour and spirit of the Dominion of Canada. We found it everywhere. It was a little difficult to analyse, but I think that it owed much of its force to a belief that the soldiers of the United States could do what Canadians have done, and to a great pride that soldiers, coming from the same Continent, largely from the same stock, had won for their armies so much martial glory.

Once for all, I make my apology for the informal and often disconnected character of the pages that follow, expressing, however, in extenuation the view that, if I succeed in conveying to my countrymen even one hundredth part of the determination of the people of the United States, it will have been worth my while to write these pages and (a much more hardy claim) worth their while to glance through them.

FREDERICK SMITH.

CONTENTS

APPENDICES

ILLUSTRATIONS

MY AMERICAN VISIT

CHAPTER I

WE reached Liverpool at 10.30 p.m. on Monday, the 17th of December, and went to the new Adelphi Hotel. It is very magnificent, though less homely than the old hotel, which has been my headquarters in so many elections. But the old atmosphere was preserved by many old and faithful friends among the servants. We did not at this moment know either the hour of the steamer's departure, or even the date of its sailing.

We met at the hotel Sir Charles Gordon, Vice-President of the Bank of Montreal, and Lord Northcliffe's principal assistant in his American Mission. He is a man with a very sleepy manner, but a very vigilant brain. I had met and liked him at Lord

Beaverbrook's, and he was destined to become a close friend. Mr. Lamont, of the firm of J. P. Morgan & Co., was also at the hotel. The services this gentleman has rendered to Great Britain, and the warmth of his sympathy with the Allied cause, are well known to all who have during the war been concerned with the relations between Great Britain and the United States. Here also there came to see us my old and faithful friend, Alderman Sir Archibald Salvidge, whom I have met very often in the same hotel, on quite different business.

We were to sail on a famous vessel, the name of which *non est dicere versu*. At 10.45 we saw the Marine Transport Officer and learnt that the ship would leave the Gladstone Dock at 11.45 a.m. This dock is some five or six miles down the river, so three taxis hurriedly left the Adelphi Hotel and our journey had begun.

It was strange to travel in so large a ship and find it so empty. There were available for quite ordinary passengers rooms which, in the happy days before the war, would have been possible only for very rich men.

Almost as soon as we reached the ship

we moved into the stream, and destroyers which were to protect us came alongside. The officers dined on board with us, and after dinner we talked of everything, from the North Sea to the Persian Gulf and the Tigris. I fear the censorship (partly because I am responsible for so many of its prosecutions), and therefore, without mentioning his name,* I add that one of the officers was the hero of the *Firefly* episode on the Tigris, when his gun-boat was shelled and captured by the Turks, he himself being hit in twenty-three different places by shell fragments. A strange chance arranged long afterwards, when many hospitals had patched him up, that he should recapture his own ship. The same officer was serving on a destroyer in the North Sea when its bridge was carried clean over the funnels and deposited aft. He and his captain were swept away with it. The captain, I fancy, was killed, the officer in question escaped with broken fingers. His nerves and spirits seemed quite un-affected, and he contributed greatly to a most agreeable evening.

* I confess that I have never understood the professional objection to disclosing the names of individuals who have rendered gallant service.

At 2 p.m. the voyage began, our escort having been considerably increased.

I have said that the ship was very empty. Besides Sir Charles Gordon and Mr. Lamont, we found on board Mr. Beekman, Governor of Rhode Island, and Mrs. Beekman; Miss Collis, a lady doctor on her way to lecture at Toronto University, thereby relieving a professor for other work; Mr. George Whitney. Colonel Boyce Thompson, the United States Red Cross Commissioner in Russia, fresh from Petrograd and much more full of enthusiasm for Kerensky than I was myself, He was extremely well known in business circles in New York, and was given a military commission in order to assist him in his work. Out of his own private resources he had made vast contributions to the necessities of Russia. And among our number was Lieut.-Col. McCuig, D.S.O., 13th Canadian Infantry, who has been through everything from the second battle of Ypres in April, 1915, to the Vimy Ridge and Paschendaele, suffering two wounds in his time. This is his first leave home during a period of service of two years and eight months. He is known as one of the most gallant and competent officers of the Canadian forces.

His brother, now a prisoner in Germany, was the hero of the stirring episode related in the first volume of Lord Beaverbrook's " Canada in Flanders." He was dangerously wounded in the second battle of Ypres, and was reported dead, but was afterwards found to have been captured.

Later in the afternoon the wind freshened ; even our mighty ship felt its effect ; and our destroyers began to make heavy weather of it. It was about this time that air-ships, shining like silver cylinders in the sun, added their friendly solicitude. And so we sailed on ; the destroyers on each side, puissant symbols of the ancient sea power of Great Britain, our own vessel ploughing a majestic course through the purple sea, the enchanting coast-line of Ireland on our beam, and the shimmering air-boats glittering in the wintry sun. It was hard to realize that we were in a danger zone.

All voyages in peace time are much the same, and most people, in these unhappy days, understand the day to day life of a war voyage. It is, therefore, not proposed to attempt any detailed description of this stage in our mission. The larger rooms in the ship had been appropriated to war purposes. We dined, therefore, a small but friendly company, in the Second-Class Dining Saloon. We talked a great deal. We played bridge. As I expected to make about thirty speeches, and was anxious as far as possible not to repeat myself, I gave as much time and thought as I could to the interminable rhetoric which lay in front of me. For exercise the gymnasium sufficed. And as I bored myself for an hour a day on the back of the trotting ostrich, or pedalled on that bicycle which never reached its goal, I comforted myself by the recollection (daily and publicly dwelt upon by the instructor) that the far more dignified form of Mr. Arthur Balfour had submitted to the same indignities in the same cause.

The weather was quite wonderful throughout. Nearly every day brought brilliant sunshine, and I myself never wore a great coat during the whole voyage. A hazy atmosphere was almost constant, and the refracted rays of the sun made beautiful effects in the water. At times a rainbow of surpassing beauty girdled the whole sky. And once its aerial hemisphere was reflected, so as to complete the circle, in the red sea, just as the sun set. And lo! the ship was actually threading its way through a perfect circle of prismatic loveliness. The oldest sailor on board had never seen an appearance quite so beautiful.

At intervals there was big gun practice at targets dropped from the ship. All our little world went to see them, and we were much encouraged by seeing the accuracy of the shooting at long distance targets. It was strange to see the great geysers of water springing up so high, as the shells fell in rapid succession. And every shell was close to the target.

The chief excitement on board was now the question whether we should eat our Christmas dinner in New York or not. In fact we were to do so. Modest as it was, we had our sweepstake. I never won one in my life and was not to be more fortunate now.

After long waiting for the slack of the tide, we were docked, not without the help of many tugs (some pulling, others pushing or butting) in the White Star dock. It was most bitterly cold.

So the voyage ended. We cannot part from this famous and fortunate ship, which has twice beaten off U-boat attacks, without rendering public thanks to its gallant and experienced Captain, in whom the crew so passionately believe that they smile even at the sea perils of this war.

May she always be as happy in the future !

CHAPTER II

IT was good to see again the Statue of Liberty and the tall sky-scrapers; to breathe in the hard, clear, glittering atmosphere of New York, and, above all, to realize that all its greatness, all its wealth, all its resources, and all its energies were harnessed to our allied purposes. Usually, the impressiveness and bustle of New York sound to me a note of aloofness, but the moment we landed, we experienced a feeling which never left us during our stay, that the United States had wholly altered. We were no longer alien travellers " exposed " to custom officers, as the Duke of Wellington said of himself in relation to authors. Every incident suggested war. The landing stage was protected by armed sentries. We were received with almost bewildering courtesy by a custom house officer, who very genially refused

9

to examine our baggage, and there, waiting for us, was Mr. Geoffrey Butler, a member of the famous Cambridge family, who is Colonel John Buchan's representative in America. Suave, bland, tactful, methodical, very much a man of the world, he is an ideal representative of this branch of our diplomatic activity. He made all the complicated arrangements for our various tours. Never has the American railway service been so completely dislocated. Never has the American climate behaved quite so vilely. Yet not once did we miss an engagement in our far-flung travels.

We were met with a disappointment. I particularly wished, and had been most urgently invited, to speak at San Francisco. But it was impossible. The New York Bar Association Address and the Ohio Banquet, which were my principal engagements, had been arranged for the middle of January. I had a most important case to argue in the Prize Court on the 17th of February, and the margin of time was hopelessly insufficient.

Rooms had been taken for us at the Plaza Hotel. I had previously stayed at the " Ritz-Carlton," but it was decided that recent associations made a change desirable.

It is well known that the late German Ambassador and his staff had made the "Ritz-Carlton" their headquarters in New York. Let me say at once that at no hotel in the world can the traveller be made to feel more completely at home than at the "Plaza." Everyone, from the manager who received us, to the boy who "paged" us, conspired to spoil us. And the porter is a Yorkshireman, and therefore (as he observed) able to despise alike in winter and summer the varying menaces of the New York climate. He added, being evidently a literary man, that anyone who could stand the climate of "Wuthering Heights" could support anything which could be produced in the United States.

It was decided for the first tour, which ended on the 10th January, to follow without alteration the programme suggested by Butler and to ask Sir Charles Gordon and Lt.-Colonel Harold Henderson, Military Secretary to his Excellency the Governor, to arrange the Canadian visit. They asked me how many speeches I would make. I said, "As many as you think useful." I had sketched out on the boat the material for about thirty speeches of kinds. The first

instalment of the programme was formidable
enough.   It was as follows :

Leave			Arrive.		
New York	Dec. 28th,	Midnight.	Washington	Dec. 29th,	7.30 a.m.
Washington	Jan. 1st,	5.40 p.m.	Cincinnati	Jan. 2nd,	6.35 a.m.
Cincinnati	,, 3rd,	9.5 p.m.	St. Louis	,, 4th,	7.30 a.m.
St. Louis	,, 5th,	11.59 p.m.	Chicago	,, 6th,	7.40 a.m.
Chicago	,, 7th,	11.45 p.m.	Detroit	,, 8th,	8.0 a.m.
Detroit	,, 8th,	11.0 p.m.	Cleveland	,, 9th,	7.45 a.m.
Cleveland	,, 10th,	7.30 a.m.	New York	,, 10th,	10.10 p.m.

I now take two pages from the diary.

Tuesday, Christmas Day.—We dined quietly
at the hotel.   The dining-room was crowded,
and everyone eating turkey and plum pud-
ding.   A good Christmas atmosphere.   Tom
Chadbourne, one of the most successful
lawyers in the States, now doing war work
at Washington (I suppose at the tariff rate—
a dollar a year), an old English friend, came
in to see us.   He is inviting the most
important business men of Wall Street, or
as many as he can collect on short notice,
to meet us at dinner before we start.   He has
asked one hundred people.

Wednesday, December 26th.—We went in
the morning down town to the Morgan offices
and met most of the partners.   We then
went to lunch with the members of the

Northcliffe Mission and were " put wise " by them on many points which are difficult to strangers. We had a long and very useful talk. Then to the Racquet Club, where I had a Turkish bath, and afterwards to the " Metropolitan," the magnificent building not far from the " Plaza."

We dined with my old Newport friends, the Pembroke-Jones'—a delightful dinner in a most beautiful house. Later we went to see Miss Maxine Elliott in *Lord and Lady Algie*. I thought her better in her part than in any in which I had seen her. We took her to supper afterwards at the Cocoanut Grove, where there was beautiful Spanish dancing, much general gaiety, and very little atmosphere of the war. Ben Ali Haggin, the distinguished artist, and his wife, were of the party, which was very amusing.

Thursday, December 27th.—We lunched at the Bankers' Club, on the forty-second storey, with the American Pilgrims, where I had been asked to make a speech. That splendid veteran, Mr. Chauncey Depew, was present and many other lawyers, judges and business men. Mr. Depew is now eighty-three. He delivered a speech full of fire and vigour, the effect of which was much increased by the distinction of his personality. James Beck spoke as always with great force and literary charm. I was asked to speak, and did so, for thirty minutes. The spirit shown by all the speakers was admirable and the way in which they spoke of Great Britain and her efforts almost brought the tears to one's eyes.

We dined with Sir Charles Gordon at the " Ritz-Carlton." We then went to the Century Theatre to meet an old friend in Miss Elsie Janis, who had sent us a box and whom I had met often in London in the old days when poor Basil Hallam was alive. After the play, we took her out to supper— Sir Charles Gordon, Mrs. Janis, Miss Elsie and the three of us—a pleasant and varied day.

Next morning Chadbourne, who, in the phrase used here, is a strong " administration " man, took us to see Colonel House by appointment. I had twice been accidentally prevented from meeting this remarkable man on his recent visit to England, and was very anxious to make his acquaintance. His influence in this country is certainly very extraordinary, and his position a very unusual

one. I had recently read in a hostile paper
the amusing criticism : " In politics the
Colonel is no pussyfoot." However that
may be, he is in private life a gentleman
of quiet and charming address, and he
received us with the greatest civility and good
nature.

I cannot, being unable, under existing
conditions, to consult his wishes, presume
to set forth any part of the conversation. I
regret this circumstance very much, for all
he said was marked by great sagacity and
persuasiveness.

We felt, after half an hour, that we had
made sufficient demands upon the time of
this very busy man, and accordingly took our
leave. The thoughtfulness of his views, and
his quiet expression of them, were very
striking ; and I went away feeling that
it was not difficult to understand how
he had attained to a position of such
authority.

Friday, December 28*th*, 1917.—In the
morning, we visited the Stock Exchange,
where extraordinary sensations and excite-
ments were in progress, caused by the action
of the Government in taking over the rail-
roads. It was wilder than ever, and, as

always in these bewildering surroundings, I found the pandemonium alarming. It was quite impossible to hear oneself speak. Even the President, who was most good-natured in explaining things, said it was unusual.

We had a very interesting lunch with the Morgan partners. Many illuminating explanations of things over here—all agree that the spirit of the country is splendid, and that it is improving daily, but the definiteness of the warnings not to expect too much too quickly is a little depressing. Later experience, however, satisfied us that they were well founded. The truth is that the United States have undertaken simultaneously a number of tasks, each of which is so stupendous that even their gigantic energy must prove slower in its fruits than was hoped. Food organization and supplies; financial co-ordination; ship-building, naval and mercantile; the raising and equipping of gigantic armies; the construction upon an immense scale of aeroplanes; such are the tasks which call for effort at the same moment.

It is only necessary to state the number of these problems to realize the necessity of patience.

We were all impressed by Stettinius, who has since, apparently, been put in charge of munitions, and who, by universal consent, is a man of quite extraordinary power. We had a long and most interesting talk with many of the partners. No alcohol was served with the meal, an omission often to be repeated, to which my secretaries never became reconciled, though they were to become familiar with it. I shall examine this question more thoroughly later.

To-night was the night for Chadbourne's banquet at Sherry's. It certainly was a most amazing assembly if measured by the importance of the guests, who, numbering ninety-two, sat around the vast table, and represented I know not how much wealth, learning and importance. I was told, but do not precisely remember, how many judges, heads of banks, railways and great financial establishments were present. I was so alarmed that I surrendered at once and delivered to them a speech which I had intended for the first meeting of five or six thousand. Their kindness and enthusiasm were so great as quite to carry one away. They stood up several times, cheered loudly in the course of it, and altogether showed so

much warmth that I was much affected.
Of course, we had always known that New
York and the East generally was with us.
But I had not realized that Wall Street was
quite so enthusiastic.

James M. Beck, a valiant friend of ours in
the old days, author of " The Evidence
in the Case," and of many mordant
phrases which will live, made a most excellent speech, and Mitchell, the out-going
Mayor of New York, sat on the other side
of our host. He is young, distinguished-
looking, and, I am told, one of the most
capable administrators New York has ever
had. He is trying to obtain (and has since
obtained) a commission in the United States
Army. And amongst the guests was John
S. Stanchfield, of whom nearly everyone
agreed that he was the best " trial lawyer "
or advocate in the States. He was untiring
in his offers of kindness. And here we met
for the first time Charles Blair McDonald,
the banker, to whom I had a letter of introduction from my friend and Parliamentary
Secretary, Urban Broughton, the Member
for Preston, and who was to prove one of
the warmest of our friends.

The table was exquisitely decorated with

orchids and the dinner very good, but not extravagant.

The meeting broke up rather in a panic, as it was suddenly announced that our train for Washington left at 11.30 and it was then 11. It seemed at first as if we were in some difficulty, as none of our boxes was packed. It turned out, however, that we could catch the same train an hour or so later by crossing the river to Liberty Street. This we did in intense cold, the thermometer being many degrees below zero, and found ourselves in the first American railway car of the tour.

CHAPTER III

THE ATTITUDE AND FEELING OF THE UNITED STATES TOWARDS THE WAR, AS ILLUSTRATED BY PROHIBITION AND OTHER MATTERS

I BREAK off from the diary to discuss, amongst other matters, a question full of interest at this moment to almost every civilized country, and one which throws a great light upon the spirit in which the American nation approaches the war; that of the prohibition during war-time of the sale, the importation and even the use of alcohol.

To this discussion I add some observations which we made quite early, and which were not afterwards disturbed, as to the general war atmosphere of the United States, which is, of course, largely responsible for the policy which has been adopted in this and other cognate matters.

On previous visits I had, as was natural, experience of dry States; and the newspapers had recently made it plain that both in the United States and in Canada the dry movement was growing very rapidly, but I certainly was not prepared for the very great development both in opinion and in practice which I found. New York, of course, is not dry, nor do I think that it would be easy to make it so, though even here I speak cautiously, in view of many surprising experiences. But Washington is dry, in the sense that no hotel and no club may supply alcoholic drink. It is not, however, dry in the sense that private hosts, even those occupying high public positions, feel called upon to withdraw it from their tables. But no stranger going to Washington without private introductions could, by any means of which I was informed, obtain any alcohol at all ; and we were later to travel through great areas where the same rules prevailed. Very often even the strictest system was enforced, and severe penalties were imposed upon any person who imported alcohol into the prohibited area. The Attorney-General of one of the States gave me a list of the number of cases in which he had prosecuted. I cannot remember the total, but it was very considerable. He told me that as a result the importation of alcohol had almost ceased. In such cases the inhabitants were allowed to consume their existing stocks, but there was, of course, no means whatever of replenishing them.

The same developments have taken place in Canada, so that to-day the whole of Canada is dry in one or other of the degrees explained above, except the Province of Quebec, which is closely threatened. Ottawa, like Washington, is dry, including as the result, of course, of his voluntary decision, the house of His Excellency the Governor-General, whose hospitable cellars have been sealed. But just across the river is the town of Hull in the Province of Quebec, and a little further out than Hull is the country club, to which so many people in Ottawa belong. At present, therefore, anyone in Ottawa who wants alcohol can be indulged at the expense of a very short journey.*

The complete, or almost complete, withdrawal from such large numbers of people of a drug, which for good or bad has been so notorious and so popular, is a phenomenon of which I always attempted to note the results.

The contest is, in fact, as old as any in the history of the human race. It is founded

* While this work is passing through the press the news arrives that the manufacture of alcohol will be absolutely prohibited in Canada after April 1st of the present year.

upon the eternal distinction between those
who are by temperament, and habit, ascetic
and those who are of an easier habit. On the
one hand, many excellent citizens lay stress
upon the evils which attend upon the abuse
of alcohol—the vice, the crime, the ruin, moral
and often physical, of weak persons. The case
is a powerful one. Their opponents reply that
the abuse of a delightful drug by weak persons
affords no justification for denying its use to
persons of self-control. How will this controversy end ? Is it destined to spread all over
the world ? Will the creed of severity prove
too strong for the philosophy of Nishapour *
—which Fitzgerald paraphrased :

> " Ah, fill the cup :—what boots it to repeat
>   How time is slipping underneath our feet :
> Unborn to-morrow, and dead yesterday,
>   Why fret about them if to-day be sweet ! "

And which John Payne illustrated in his
translation of another quatrain :

> " With a fair-faced maid and wine rose-red by the stream-
>   let's brink,
> Of ease and leisure I'll take my pleasure nor pause to
>   think.
> I was not aye : but am to day and yet will be.
> I've drunk of yore, and drink e'ermore, and yet will
>   drink."

* It may be usefully noted that Omar Khayyám lived
(according to the best tradition) to his hundredth year.

The forces deploying for this great social antagonism are not unequally matched. It will be interesting to study the final result of their collision.

I came to the same conclusion both as regards the United States and Canada, and, therefore, the subject of the two countries may be treated together. I ought to say that I started with the strong belief that in these countries large bodies of men would not permanently submit to prohibition. It is too soon yet to predict with confidence whether or not a reaction will follow upon the present very remarkable movement. But I have seen many things which have very much surprised me, and which lead me to think it by no means improbable that in these two countries the movement may become almost or quite general, and may permanently, or for a long time, succeed.

In the United States we frequently addressed what are known as Rotary Clubs at the luncheon hour. Such a club is one consisting of members selected almost from every known profession, trade or industry in the place. It contains, therefore, a large number of interesting and versatile people, and on great occasions six or seven hundred people will assemble at their public functions. In Canada luncheons of a similar kind are given by what are known as the various Canadian Clubs, the members of which are not selected so as to represent different trades, but are chosen as public-spirited citizens, who meet at lunch to discuss or hear addresses from strangers upon matters which concern Canada.   I have known the audience at a Canadian Club luncheon number as many as a thousand.   Neither at the Rotary Clubs nor at the Canadian Clubs is any alcohol served or permitted.   And I am bound to say, though not a specially friendly critic (for I do not like the system), that none of the members seemed very much to resent the drought, and that their abstinence in no way diminished the warmth of their en-thusiasm.   Indeed, I think it only fair to state that I derived the impression from all those luncheons that the majority of those present had accustomed themselves quite easily to abstention from alcohol.   The sub-ject was seldom raised unless one started it oneself.

The same observation must be made in reference to the large dinners of lawyers, or Chambers of Commerce, at which we were entertained both in the United States and in the Dominion. Everywhere we saw long tables, able, perhaps, to seat eight hundred guests, with hundreds of glasses of water containing lumps of ice.

In the main I cannot say that the majority of those present seemed to suffer any inconvenience, or even to be conscious of any deprivation. I do indeed remember that my host in one city before the dinner offered me a cocktail, which I accepted. We went downstairs to the American bar, and there certainly saw some slight congestion of those who were to meet us later at the dry dinner. And I was told on high authority that a few farmers of the West in dry districts, by applying a cream separator to the processes of brewing cider, are able to extract a pure alcohol which is thirty per cent. stronger than ordinary brandy. I heard this from a knowledgeable person, but am not able to confirm it from observation. I was also told that the people of the Kansas City which is dry, sometimes made excursions into the Kansas City which is wet, but I cannot remember any other qualifications to the general view I formed that hundreds of lawyers and business men, after long days of hard work, were apparently content to dine without alcohol, and yet exhibited, during and after their meal, great cordiality and enthusiasm.

It is very difficult to make any prediction about the future. Before I reached the United States I should have rejected as utterly incredible the view that the whole of the United States could ever become dry. To-day I am less confident. It is still necessary to be cautious in prediction. Immense forces will be required to bring the drink traffic to an end in such places as New York, San Francisco and Chicago, and even if such a change be successfully imposed for the moment, it is, in my judgment, uncertain whether it could be maintained, without serious and perhaps general reactions.

I have said that the same general observations apply to Canada. The task of extending the area of prohibition in the Dominion has been rendered easier by the formation of the Coalition Government, because the Liberal members are all vehemently in favour of it, and their influence has proved decisive. I cannot state of the two countries any decided conclusion, but it is right that I should add that it seems to me far more probable, than

I could ever have believed, that both these
countries will in the near future become
what in the current phrase is known as
" bone dry."

It is at least certain that the prohibitionists
in both countries have made a most successful use of the war to support their campaign.
And those affected by it (I had almost said
their victims) do not appear greatly to
resent it, or to be preparing an effective
counter-campaign. I must in fairness add
that I hardly saw an intoxicated person in
either the United States or the Dominion.

It is not inconvenient, before resuming
my diary, that I should make in this place a
few other general observations upon the
outward appearance of things in the United
States. One is always being asked " Do the
Americans realize how grave the war is ? "
Or " What signs are outwardly observable
that America is at war ? " One might, on
first walking down Broadway, reply, perhaps
superficially, that there is little enough to
meet the eye which speaks of war. There
is far, far less khaki than one meets in London. The street lights and the illuminated
advertisements are still strangely brilliant
to our London eyes, though the latter have

been greatly curtailed, and the former, in most American towns, are lowered once or twice a week. The streets of New York and of all the principal towns are alive with automobiles of every type and size. All were driven by men. This, one would suppose, can hardly last indefinitely. Every capable chauffeur is a mechanic or can readily be made one, and this class of men, consisting of hundreds of thousands of individuals, could evidently be used, and indeed cannot long be dispensed with, in some branch or other of the public service. The outward emblem, most constantly in evidence, of the war is the Red Cross, which is found in nearly every window. A subscription of a dollar entitles the subscriber to exhibit the badge in his window. And so the Red Cross badge, from the palace to the hovel, has almost become the symbol of loyalty to the common cause.

I have been asked whether economy of food is gaining ground in the United States. I am sure that it is, though slowly. Certainly the authorities are making the most strenuous efforts by precept and example to induce a more sparing consumption of foodstuffs. There are wheatless days, meatless days and pigless days, nor should the extraordinarily stringent coal order be forgotten. This order was naturally the subject of much criticism, but it certainly brought the war home to a great many people. And I found in the United States many complaints from people who were unable to warm their houses properly.

I ought, I think, to call attention to a very weighty statement made to me by one of the great authorities at Washington, to the effect that the population of Great Britain was to-day consuming more food per head of the population than before the war.* He explained this circumstance by the high wages ruling at home, and he supported it by a wealth of figures and statistics, which I had no means of testing or confuting. But as he was a very experienced man, and was pointing out the vital importance of economy in Great Britain in order that public opinion in the States might be satisfied, it is worth while noting his conclusion. And I observed that many of the Hearst papers, finding a difficulty in continuing the anti-war campaign in the present state of public

---

* This was, of course, written before our adoption of the rationing system.

opinion, were adopting the specious headline of "America First," supporting their arguments by a supposed degree of luxury which they imputed to the European Allies of the United States of America.

These suggestions may now be examined and corrected in the light of Mr. Hoover's evidence, given on February 17th before the Committee on Agriculture of the House of Representatives.

He stated that in 1916 the American people consumed ten per cent. more food than in 1914, which was neither a year of food shortage nor hard times, but if they would revert to the 1914 conditions that difference of ten per cent. will meet the Allied requirements. For instance, to give the Allies the wheat they need the Americans would have to curtail their consumption by about 100,000,000 bushels, which could be made up by the use chiefly of maize meal. The estimated Allied requirements of beef from January to July 1st were 45,000,000 pounds. The ordinary American surplus was 50,000,000 pounds, so the difference must be made up by a saving of about ten per cent. While the American has been eating more in the last two years, the Englishman and

Frenchman, according to Mr. Hoover, has been eating about thirty per cent. less than the normal quantity.

The difficulty in sending food supplies to the Allies has not been, according to this high authority, the submarines or the scarcity of ships, but the shortage of railway cars and the congestion on the railway systems. Of all the foodstuffs shipped from America to Europe, Mr. Hoover told the Committee, the submarines get only from five to seven per cent., but in the last three months the railways supplied 100,000 fewer cars for grain transportation than they did in the corresponding period of last year, and this actual decrease was still further reduced by the length of time required to move the cars owing to weather conditions.

The external signs that the United States are at war are already numerous and multiply daily. They have submitted, and are daily submitting, to the exercise of the most extraordinary powers by the Executive. But the indications derived from contact with American humanity, and hereafter to be described, are so overwhelmingly clear, that those indications which merely meet the eye in the streets, or are otherwise superficially encountered, need not be further considered.

Perhaps the circumstance of all others which brought home to the travellers the abnormal nature of the times was the Government's control over the railways and the extraordinarily drastic measures, referred to above, which it was found necessary to take in order to deal with the coal situation.

It would be almost impossible to describe the unpunctuality and dislocation of the train service during our travels. It is hardly an exaggeration to say that every train was late, and most of them hours late. It is no doubt true that the abnormal weather conditions prevailing contributed to this result, but it cannot seriously be disputed that far more permanent causes were at work. The purposes of war demand the closest co-ordination among railway systems, but the deliberate policy of successive administrations at Washington, in the reaction from omnipotent combinations, has been to compel all round competition. Where the heads of railways have for years been compelled to compete and forbidden to co-ordinate, you cannot expect in one moment to find among them either the willingness or the power to

3

co-ordinate, and I was told by more than one railway official of great experience that the financial policy of administration in relation to the railways had made it difficult for the companies to keep their rolling stock and locomotives up to a reasonable pitch of efficiency. I do not pretend to know the rights and wrongs of this controversy, and only repeat the view as it was put before me, but it was certainly true that the method of control by individual companies had completely broken down, when Mr. Secretary McAdoo was put in charge of the Government Department which took them over. Most people agreed that the railway chaos was the chief cause of the shortage of fuel. The remedy ultimately adopted by the Government shows how desperate the crisis had become. It was decided to close down on certain days every non-war factory, store, office and place of business, thus leaving the plant and work-people idle, in order to effect an immediate and general economy of fuel. This very drastic remedy was bitterly resisted at Washington and much criticized in the Press. But it seemed to me on the whole that the country was convinced of the necessity of the steps taken, and was prepared to acquiesce in what was admittedly a very extreme demand. The example set by the United States has since been followed in Canada. The patience with which both countries have supported this and other inconveniences of the gravest kind are of happy augury for their future demeanour in this most exacting war.

CHAPTER IV

WASHINGTON — THE EMBASSY — INTERVIEWS
WITH MINISTERS AND WITH THE PRESIDENT

I RETURN to the diary.

Saturday, December 29th.—We arrived at
Washington at 12.15 p.m., four and a half
hours late. The Ambassador and Lady
Spring-Rice most kindly asked H. S. and
myself to stay at the Embassy. The Colonel
stayed with Sir Charles Gordon.

I had not met Sir Cecil or Lady Spring-
Rice before. They showed us the greatest
kindness, and that most precious form of
hospitality which allows the guest to do
whatever he wishes. I knew, of course, by
reading his dispatches, for two and a half
years, of the extraordinary difficulties with
which Sir Cecil had been confronted during
the period before the United States entered
the war ; but I carried away from many

long and intimate talks with him a far deeper and more vivid impression of the pitfalls amid which he daily walked. The course pursued, and I think necessarily and wisely pursued, by President Wilson involved all those, who were diplomatically concerned, in a situation requiring the daily exhibition of tact, subtlety and patience. I gladly place on record the tribute rendered to our Ambassador by a Cabinet Minister of great sagacity : " No man ever had a more diffi- cult hand to play ; no man ever played it with fewer positive errors." He gave me the impression of a man who had felt the strain of his labours and responsibility.* But he was always willing to talk, to help and to advise, and I owed much in my visit to his wise counsel. It is a pleasure to put on record my view that he has rendered services of the highest character to his country, during a most anxious and critical period.*

We found on our arrival that our host and hostess were dining out, but Lieut.-Colonel

* These words were written by me before I heard of the melancholy and premature death of our late Ambassador. I have not altered nor added to them, though I would have used a warmer note could I have read the future. He died for England as certainly as if he had perished in the trenches. He was a very sincere, able and patriotic Englishman.

Arthur Murray, M.P., brother of my old friend Lord Elibank, had most kindly arranged a dinner for us, at which he and Mr. Arthur Willert, of the British War Mission, were joint hosts. We dined at the Metropolitan Club at eight o'clock ; many interesting people were present, including Mr. Redfield, the Secretary of Commerce ; Mr. Houston, the Secretary of Agriculture ; Mr. Hurley, the Chairman of the Shipping Board ; and Mr. Phillips, the Assistant Secretary of State. Major Harold Baker, M.P., and my colleague at the Bar, Mr. Mitchell Innes, K.C., who has given up his practice for the public service, were also of the party. General McLachlin and General Trotter represented the soldiers, Commodore Grant, R.N. the sailors.

We had a great deal of interesting talk, both in general and particular. I sat between Redfield and Houston, and later in the evening, we changed places, so as to make the acquaintance of everyone. The Ministers were very frank, talking quite without reserve. Houston particularly showed a great knowledge of agricultural problems in Europe. He spoke of the growing needs of the next few months and distinguished very clearly between the measures which were desirable and those which were possible. I was much struck by Phillips, the Assistant Secretary of State, who seemed a very clever and attractive man. Everyone spoke in the highest possible terms of the soldiers whom we had sent to the United States. The junior officers sent as instructors had made a particularly good impression. I may mention that wherever we travelled we heard the same report. Let me add here in a later note that Colonel Ericcson, the officer commanding U.S.A. troops on the ship which brings us home, told me that in his division he had four British officers who did the work of forty, and were adored by everyone.

So ended a very interesting evening.

Sunday, December 30th.—It is bitterly cold, the frost being intense. In the morning, we called on Chief Justice White at his house ; he received us with the greatest kindness. Well over seventy years old, he presides with equal dignity and learning over the Supreme Court. He is an old admirer of Great Britain, and moved us very much by his tribute to the efforts our country had made in the war. He questioned us very closely about conditions in England and asked very

earnestly, " Will they see it out ? Will
that old British spirit hold in all these suffer-
ings ? "   He told us with sincere and friendly
emphasis how completely he had been with
us since August, 1914. And more than
once he said with old-fashioned warmth :
" I wish you could have broken bread with
me." We left him, carrying in our minds
the impression of a splendid veteran, a courtly
gentleman of the old school, and a very
sagacious lawyer. We then called on the
Attorney-General, but were not fortunate
enough to find him in.   We lunched with Sir
Charles Gordon, and in the afternoon by
appointment, at 3.30, Mr. Secretary Lane
and Senator B. Kellogg called, and stayed for
an hour and a half, smoking and talking.
Lane is a very genial and amusing man, with
a keen sense of humour.   We talked about
conditions in the United States and Great
Britain.   Much that was said can, naturally,
not be repeated, but Lane was very informing about the tonnage problem.   He asked
whether I would like him to accompany me
on the second part of my tour—a proposal
which was naturally very agreeable to me.

In the evening the Ambassador had invited
the Judges of the Supreme Court, the Law

Officers and one or two others to meet us at dinner. The guests were the Chief Justice, Mr. Justice McKenna, Mr. Justice Day, Mr. Justice Van Devanter, Mr. Justice Brandeis, Mr. Justice Clarke, Mr. Attorney-General Gregory, Mr. Solicitor-General Davis, Mr. Warren, the Assistant Attorney-General, Mr. Charles Storey, of the Department of Justice, and Mr. Mitchell Innes, K.C., of the North-Eastern Circuit.

I was very sorry that an old friend, Mr. Justice Oliver Wendell Holmes, was prevented from being present. I have always thought that his work on " The Common Law " is one of the most profound studies of the principles which underly our legal system. I had last seen him at a small fancy dress dance and dinner at my house at Charlton in 1912.

I was naturally very glad to meet so many members of one of the greatest judicial bodies in the world. I sat between the Chief Justice and Mr. Justice Brandeis, the most recently appointed judge, and evidently an extremely clever man. Afterwards we changed places, and I had a long talk with my colleague, the Attorney-General. Here, and later with the Solicitor-General, I was able to discuss many matters of interest to both countries, which are not easy to arrange by correspondence.

The relative positions of the Attorney-General and the Solicitor-General in the United States are by no means the same as in England. The Attorney-General over here is so much absorbed in that kind of administrative work, which in continental countries falls to the Minister of Justice, that he seldom, or never, argues a case in Court himself. The most important cases which require the appearance of law officers are the appeals to the Supreme Court, and practically the whole of these, in cases affecting the Government, are argued by the Solicitor-General. The first or second Assistant Attorney-General is available to help him in matters requiring the presence of more than one Counsel.

The Attorney is a very pleasant and agreeable man, and full of explanation about American legal affairs. He was most anxious, as the Chief Justice had been, to arrange a dinner for the Bar to meet me before we left Washington. But unfortunately it was not possible. He is very highly spoken of as an administrator.

The Solicitor-General enjoys a great reputation as a lawyer. We spoke of the prospects and positions of law officers in the States and Great Britain, particularly in relation to salaries and the prospects of judicial promotion. It appears that in the United States law officers rarely become judges, and, on a vacancy in the office of Attorney-General, the Solicitor-General is not often given the office. Salaries seem ludicrously low in the United States, and I was told by many lawyers, who had been either Attorney or Solicitor, of cases where men had held the office for a short time, in order to gain prestige in their profession, and had then prematurely, to the prejudice of the public service, given it up in order to make nine or ten times as much in private practice.

The Chief Justice explained to me how much their method of trying a legal argument differs from ours. Each side, as is well known, prepares elaborate written briefs, containing a full citation of the relevant authorities. When the case comes before the Court the advocates present an attractive, and comparatively short, summary of their written briefs. The Court almost always postpones its decision, the draft of which is prepared by one of the judges " assigned " for that purpose by the Chief Justice. I said that on the whole our methods seem to make a greater demand upon the ability of the Bar and perhaps even of the Bench. I fancy that he agreed.

Monday, December 31*st.*—At 10 a.m. there was an instructive conference at the Embassy of all the heads of the various British Missions then in Washington. Those present were about ten in number, including myself and H. S., who were invited to be present. A useful and business-like talk followed. The only actual decision I recall was that British officers in uniform were not to be served with alcoholic drinks in public places in the United States. The decision was reached on the ground that it was undesirable to have one rule for British officers and a different one for Americans. It fell upon me to communicate it to the Colonel.

The Ambassador had arranged to present me to-day to the President, and other Cabinet Ministers, and accordingly took me to the Government offices in the morning. All the Ministers whom I saw were very frank, and discussed the war situation with great freedom. It is obvious that very little of the conversation can be repeated here, but I may place on record some fugitive impressions of the remarkable men who are carrying on the war in the United States. I was first taken to Mr. Secretary Lansing, who is, of course, responsible for Foreign Affairs, and who gave me the impression of a shrewd, able, self-contained man of the world; courteous and by no means without humour. We discussed the interminable question of the internal conditions of the Central Empires and Turkey. He was rather encouraging, though not extravagantly so, and his conclusions agreed very closely with those of our own Foreign Office. He was interesting about things in China, and spoke of Japan in a very generous and broad-minded manner. He was pleasant and encouraging about my tour.

I was next taken to Mr. Secretary Daniels, the Secretary for the Navy. He is a typical Southerner, with a kindly, rather whimsical face. He called in Admiral Benson, his Chief of Naval Operations, who had recently returned from Europe. Both of them, and particularly the Admiral, spoke with generous enthusiasm of our Navy. The Admiral spoke of its tactical efficiency in such a way as to make one proud. Most of our talk was of the U-boat warfare; and although Sir

Eric Geddes has recently said much the same
things to the British nation, it is better to
let those High Persons do all their own talking
in public upon these responsible topics.   And
so I shall abstain.

The next Minister in order was Mr. Secretary Baker, who is responsible for the Army,
an alert, energetic man of moderate stature,
who gave the impression of considerable
nervous energy.   Like the others, he was extremely civil and obliging, and, hearing that I
was going to Cleveland, where his constituency
is, gave me a letter to a friend of his in the
neighbourhood, a distinguished judge, whom
I afterwards met.

Baker is at present the storm centre of
all the criticism, on the ground of unprepared-
ness in military matters, which is centreing
around the Administration.   For many days
half the papers one picked up contained
leading articles which may be summarized
in the familiar letters, B.M.G.   It is well
known that in the States, Ministers are not
members of the legislative body.   They
cannot, therefore, answer in Parliament for
the Departments.   The defence of depart-
mental points is left to nominated or volunteer champions—a rôle which often affords

a great opportunity to private members. The Committees of the legislature may, and in grave matters do, require before them the attendance of a Minister. While I was in the States, Mr. Secretary Baker was twice, as it is phrased here, " put on the stand," and submitted to many hours' heckling.

Non nobis tantas componere lites, but it seemed to me, as a stranger, that the Secretary defended himself with a good deal of spirit, resource and knowledge. His critics accused him of flippancy. It is, in any event, useful in these grave and pressing matters, that there should be a constant stream of well-informed and reasonable criticism, but Mr. Secretary Baker took the line of calling attention to what had positively been achieved. And here he was on strong ground. He was greatly pressed as to why the Government had made no preparations in the fateful six months which preceded the actual breach. In my friendly judgment, his answers seemed a little less explicit in this particular. But I think he judged rightly that in this war the Present is more important than the Past and the Future than the Present.

Both Daniels and Baker had a reputation

before the war of being strong pacifists. I saw, for instance, the speech attributed in the Press to the Secretary of the Navy, only a year or two before the United States came into the war, in which he argued that there was really no need for the United States to have a strong Navy, on the ground that if they had a weak one, or none at all, every foreigner would feel it unsportsmanlike to attack a nation so defenceless. Mr. Secretary Baker, I understand, ranged himself quite clearly among those who were passionately anxious to keep America out of the war, believing, almost to the end, that tact and patience could achieve this result without prejudice to her honour and material interest. Both these gentlemen, each at the head of a belligerent department, were now completely convinced that the United States had taken the only possible choice, and that their honour and their future were bound up in the successful outcome of the war. I was told everywhere—and it would appear to be natural —that the presence in his Cabinet of two such well-known, and universally respected, pacifists, and their acquiescence in his change of policy, were of the greatest assistance to the President at the critical moment.

After a visit to Mr. Phillips, the Assistant Secretary of State, we left the building, which very conveniently contains nearly all the great public offices, and I went to White House for my interview with the President.

I had never met Mr. Wilson, and I had the kind of feeling which one always has when one is to see for the first time a man whose every public utterance it has been one's duty to read and re-read for three and a half years, and whose name is illustrious in every country in the world. With what hope, and sometimes with what disappointment, one had read his earlier speeches and Notes! And here I recall in particular his answer to the Kaiser's letter, inviting American sympathy at the very beginning of the war. And I recall, too, the long Notes, some of which I had helped to answer, in which he took up, and pressed, various points of maritime controversy with Great Britain. Then, on the other side, came the reflection of the immense difficulties which confronted the Head of a Nation so vast and so cosmopolitan in origin. A single thoughtless step, a single premature decision on the part of the Ruler, and though America might have been at war, the heart and soul of a united country

4

would not, and could not, have been claimed by its rulers for warlike purposes. Perhaps, even compulsory service and the early presence in France of the nucleus Army, with its precious message of encouragement to the French nation, would have proved impossible. And then I remembered, too, his noble utterances since the war, their insight, their Statecraft, their eloquence, their courage, and their immeasurable influence upon every free democracy in the world. And reflecting that this remarkable man had at last brought into the war a united nation, had smoothly and swiftly introduced National Service, and had mortgaged the vast industrial and financial resources of this wonderful country to the cause of the Allies, I saw how presumptuous it was for a foreigner to do anything but admire.

An atmosphere of considerable mystery, and of immense prestige, surrounds the President. He goes little into society, and functions of fashionable people interest him not at all. He sees, apparently, only a few friends, and those who are officially entitled to audience. On the other hand, when the weather allows it, he plays golf on three or four mornings in the week, and is to be found two or three times a week in a box at one of the Washington theatres. His health is delicate, and his doctor, with prudent authority, insists on these relaxations from his public anxieties.

I was received at White House by an Aide-de-Camp wearing the badge of a Colonel, and, after a few moments in an ante-room, was shown to the state room where receptions are commonly held. The President received me with great kindness and consideration, and I was with him for some twenty minutes. It would be obviously improper to recall any of his conversation upon any subject of importance, but I cannot give offence by recording the enthusiasm with which he spoke of University life, and in particular of my old University of Oxford. I spoke of his extraordinary power of divining what the American people as a whole would think of a given question. He said that in so far as he possessed it, it was, he hoped, because he was a typical American, looking at things from the same angle, and likely to reach conclusions by the same mental processes. We then spoke of his own speeches, and of those of our own Prime Minister, and after

4*

some talk about Colonel House's Mission and my own, I thought I had trespassed as long as was proper upon one whose time was so limited, and I rose to take my leave.

In the evening we dined with the Chadbournes. Among those present was Miss Wilson, a daughter of the President, who, I am told, has a wonderful voice, and sings a great deal at concerts in different parts of the States.

We went on afterwards to a ball given by Mr. and Mrs. McLean at their enormous house. Mr. McLean is proprietor of the *Washington Post*. We were told that two hundred guests sat down to dinner, and four hundred were able to dance without any overcrowding. The room was crowded with young soldiers and sailors, and it was interesting to us to see dozens of ordinary naval ratings—American young gentlemen who had flocked to the Navy—dancing with the beauties of Washington.

I met Mrs. Longworth here, daughter of ex-President Roosevelt, whom I had previously known at Newport, and I made the acquaintance of Mrs. and Miss Sally Price-Collier, the widow and daughter of the author of " England and the English."

It was a brilliant scene, and a little strange to our eyes. The hostess said, " All these boys are in the Army or Navy. They are all going, and they may be gone very soon. I am going to give them one good night." And, remembering the agony that lay in front of them, the " abhorred shears " which were to cut the threads of so many of these young lives, we rejoiced to see them happy.

CHAPTER VI

Tuesday, 1st January.—This was the day of our departure. We lunched with Mrs. Longworth, and heard some interesting talk from the Republican standpoint. This lady's social gifts are well-known, both in the States and in England. We had a delightful party.

On returning to the Embassy, we took leave of our host and hostess to catch our train for Cincinnati, which should have left at 5.40 p.m. It was our fate to wait three detestable hours at the station.

Wednesday, January 2nd.—We were due to arrive at Cincinnati at 8.40 a.m. In fact, we drew into the station at 6.15 p.m. The water was frozen in the train, and the journey altogether odious.

54

Leaving Washington.

[To face p. 54.

We were met by Mr. Shinkle, President of the Chamber of Commerce, and Judge Harmon, who was Attorney-General of the United States under President Cleveland. With a great rush, we were just able to get washed and shaved and " shined " before a dinner most hospitably given by Mr. Maxwell at the Club. About forty of the principal men of business of the town were present. I made a short speech in reply to the toast of my health. Immediately after dinner, we were taken to a great mass meeting, which was packed to the doors, and from which we were told many hundreds had been turned away. I spoke for fifty minutes. The friendliness of the audience towards us, and their enthusiasm whenever Great Britain was mentioned, exceeded belief, and at the close they cheered, standing up, both the King and Great Britain. It was the first really public meeting I had addressed, and I have not seen more enthusiasm at any public meeting since our old, far-away election days. The result reassured me greatly, for I had in my heart been anxious as to whether we should get on well with an American audience.

We drove back to our hotel, the " Sinton,"

in bitter cold and heavy snow, where we
were to have supper with Mr. and Mrs.
Shinkle. Both were charming, and took the
greatest trouble in seeing that arrangements
at the hotel were made for our comfort.

Thursday, January 3rd.—Mr. Taft, half-
brother of the late President, and his nephew
called upon us at the hotel. He invited us
to his house, where, as he modestly put it,
he had " a few things he would like us to
see." On the way to his house, he showed
us the much discussed Lincoln Statue, which
he had presented to the City of Cincinnati,
and a replica of which he had offered to
Great Britain. It is reproduced in this
volume. I am no art critic, but I thought
the condemnation of it not merely exaggerated, but, in the main, unwarrantable.
The feet, it is true, look enormous, but I
am told that, anatomically, they are in
strict proportion. Two defects struck me,
one curable, the other not. The first is that
the pedestal—about three feet high—is far
too low ; it should be, having regard to the
size of the statue, at least fifteen feet. The
second, that the pose of the arms is unhappily
conceived. It certainly lends itself to cari-
cature, but I thought that the modelling of

The much discussed statue of President Lincoln.

[To face p. 56.

that great head was marked by nobility and even by inspiration.

We then went to Mr. Taft's house, an old-fashioned, low, charming house, which had evidently once been situate in the suburbs of the town, but was now dwarfed on each side by immense factories. The kind of house, and I should think, Cincinnati, the kind of town (physically, of course, not morally) which Winston Churchill wrote of in " Inside of the Cup." In front of the house the vigilance of our host had kept a fine open space. We were very little prepared for the treasures of art which it contained. I do not think I have ever seen in one private house a collection of masterpieces with which I myself was so much delighted. On the walls, arranged with rare judgment, were Turners, Hoppners, Franz Hals, Romneys, Van Dykes and Gainsboroughs. Little as I know of art, I would gladly have spent hours amid these most enchanting surroundings.

At 12.30 we were to be the guests of one of those Rotary Clubs of which I have already spoken. The large room in which the luncheon was held was unpleasantly crowded, those present numbering five hundred and fifty.   Such an audience, as I have explained, is particularly interesting, because, by the rules of the Club, the members must be elected in rotation from every recognized trade or profession. I spoke for thirty-five minutes, which was, as they say here, according to schedule. Afterwards, the audience called on the Colonel and H.S. for short speeches.

After lunch we went for a motor drive with Shinkle, who had asked a large and most agreeable party to meet us at his house to tea. Not satisfied with the kindness he had shown us from the first moment of our arrival, this most hospitable gentleman and his wife took us to dine at a quiet and most attractive little country club called The Pillars. The cooking here was in the hands of coloured chefs, and was quite delicious.

At 9.5 p.m. we left for St. Louis, not a little grieved to leave so soon the warm-hearted friends we had met.

I break off here from the diary to make some general observations which apply to Cincinnati, St. Louis, Cleveland and Chicago, and which, therefore, may conveniently be made at this place. In every one of these cities there is a large German population, ranging from thirty to sixty per cent. I was extremely anxious to find out what was the attitude of these citizens—I am only dealing with naturalized Germans—and how far they seemed anxious to obstruct or help forward the war. I made close inquiries of the leading men in all these cities, and I put myself in touch with the Authorities who were responsible for the " draft," or Military Service Act. Great uniformity prevailed in their opinion. They all thought that the overwhelming majority of the German population was loyal and dependable. Many of them, it was pointed out, had left Prussia precisely in order to avoid the military virus which had brought this cataclysm upon the world. They still venerated, it was conceded, the spirit of Germany, but it was the old Germany. It was not the Germany which had been poisoned by those new and wicked doctrines, under the stimulus of which the whole nation was to-day staggering to ruin.

A practical proof of this, which seems to me conclusive, was furnished by the experience of those responsible for the " drafts." The German population had responded, on

the whole, as readily, and with as few claims
for exemption, as any other section of
the population, not excluding the Anglo-
Saxons. In one town, a most distinguished
American lawyer, himself of Prussian birth,
drove me round a quarter of the city which
was exclusively German. It consisted of
small, neat and wooden houses. Every house
had a Red Cross in its window. Every
house, where there were sons of the age called
up, had rendered them to the call. Two
German fathers were sitting smoking in the
downstairs room of one house we visited.
" My son," said one complacently, " is
already a corporal." " Ah," said the other,
" but mine is a sergeant. We, however,"
(this with a touch of the old Adam) " were
always a military family."

American opinion upon the point is quite
clear, and Americans are plainly the best
judges of their own problems. But the spirit
of the people is resolute to use an iron hand
with the disloyal minority. An audience of
five thousand people in Nebraska, where
also there are many Germans, stood up and
cheered for three minutes when the Governor
of the State, speaking of the Germans, and
the draft, after a tribute to those who had

joined, added, " and as for the others, let them either get in or get out."

The insolent threat, therefore, addressed by the German Chancellor to Ambassador Gerard, that grave trouble would arise among the German population if America came into the war, may be dismissed with contempt. *Solvuntur tabulae.*

Friday, January 4th.—We arrived at St. Louis at 8 a.m. and were met by Mr. Pearson, the British Consul, who took us straight to the new Statler Hotel, which, like all the Statler houses, is excellent. At ten o'clock, Judge Lee and Mr. Fay, the Secretary of the Bar Association, took us to see the Courts, where we met Judges Sambourne, Dyer, and others. I sat on the Bench and heard a naturalization case. When it was over, the presiding Judge, a fine old man eighty years old and of unimpaired powers, made a friendly speech from the Bench, welcoming me to the city.

Later in the morning, a party of judges and lawyers came to see us at the hotel to propose an improvised picnic. There certainly is a great freemasonry and quick friendliness among members of our profession. A fleet of motors was ready, and took us all to a most delightful little club, called the Log Cabin Club. Judge Priest, Judge Taylor, and Mr. Sam Fordyce were our principal hosts. It was fine and sunny and after lunch H. S. and I played golf, over links partly covered with snow, but quite playable. Later we visited the Country Club, whose members boast that they possess the greatest artist in the United States in the manufacture of cocktails. He certainly seemed very resourceful, and gave the Colonel a little book—his life's work, he added —containing two hundred different recipes for the manufacture of cocktails. St. Louis, it will be inferred, is not yet dry. But the victory was narrowly won after a desperate encounter, and the members of this and other clubs seemed a little apprehensive of the future. *Proximus Ucalegon.*

At 7.30 we were entertained at dinner by the Bar Association. Nearly six hundred members attended, of whom many were German by extraction. I was told that those present would include nearly all the legal advisers of the German population, who accept with docility the advice and cautions of their lawyers. I spoke for forty-five minutes, being told this was the period which was expected. Never, even on this visit, have we met greater kindness and enthusiasm, and I spent nearly twenty minutes at the end of the dinner, at the suggestion of the Chairman, in shaking hands with all the guests who filed past. We stayed talking and saying good-bye until 11.30. Fordyce, who is the kindest of men, observing with justice that it was always too early to go to bed, took us in a motor-car to Mr. and Mrs. Kaufmann's, where we played bridge until 2.30.

Saturday, January 5th.—Early in the morning, Judge Taylor, who, in a specially attractive way, has made himself our friend and guide, came round and took us for a walk to see the town. It was very cold, but sunny and cheerful.

We lunched for oratorical purposes at the City Club, a club, so I was told, representative of those in business, excluding in the main the employer class. It was terribly hot and crowded. The room had never before held more than six hundred, and we were told that nearly seven hundred were present, not counting those who flocked in for standing room when lunch was over. The atmosphere was quite intolerable, so that it became necessary to open some windows.

As the temperature was about zero, the
resultant ventilation was partial and disconcerting. My " scheduled " time here was
forty minutes.

After the lunch a great number of people
came to be introduced ; many of these were
from England. " I am a Lancashire lad,"
said one ; and another, " My father came from
Glasgow," a third, " They used to call me
John Bull, because I argued so much in
favour of England, but they have all got to
be John Bulls now."

I was told that the combined effect of a
dinner of the Bar Association and the City
Club was to touch almost every section of
representative society in St. Louis. After
lunch we motored round the town and visited
the Roman Catholic cathedral, which has a
magnificent high altar and a canopy of
Byzantine design. Then on to the Racquet
Club, where we met Dick Fenwick, brother of
the Fenwick who was in the Rifle Brigade
and owned that famous filly, Mimi, the
winner of the Oaks.

Judge and Mrs. Priest had invited us to
dinner at their house, a mile or two out of
town. The latter asked us whether we
realized that St. Louis contained more

Leaving St. Louis.

[To face p. 64.

beautiful ladies than any city in the States. We may, perhaps, be allowed to admit that her party afforded a very striking vindication of this bold claim.*   But ours was the fate of the Wanderers.   At eleven o'clock we left to catch the train for Chicago.

We were told in leaving that a very remarkable storm was in progress and that it was very doubtful whether we should reach Chicago.   In fact, ours was the only train which got through in twenty-four hours.

Sunday, January 6th.—We arrived at Chicago at 9 a.m., only an hour late, and were met by the Consul-General, Mr. H. Nugent.   This gentleman had passed through a most anxious and responsible time during the period of American neutrality.   He described to us in a most interesting way the German plan of campaign in Chicago : its adroitness and its extraordinary resource. And he spoke also of the constant counter exertions of our own friends.

When we left the station we found that a most virulent blizzard was blowing, and that the ground was deep in snow.   Even

* Poor Rupert Brooke wrote of the States : " Handsome people of both sexes are very common ; beautiful and pretty ones very rare."   I dissent from both these generalizations.

to us, who took abnormal weather for
granted, it seemed that the weather conditions were quite extraordinary. It was
quite impossible to walk against the storm,
and I saw many people blown from their
feet. We learnt afterwards that Chicago
had done its best for us, as this was the
heaviest combined blizzard and snow-storm
that had visited the city within living memory.
Everyone agreed that for fifty years at least
there had been no such storm.

We drove to the Blackstone Hotel, which
is claimed by Chicago citizens to be the best
in America. It is extremely good, though I
think I could mention some others, including
our Plaza, in competition. Immediately after
breakfast Mr. Samuel Insull called. He is a
very remarkable man, whose influence and
authority in Chicago are unbounded. We
were told on several hands that he controls in
one concern or another over one hundred
million sterling. He started life in England,
being a Londoner by birth. Once, in the far
away days, he was private secretary and
shorthand writer to my old friend, Mr.
Thomas Gibson Bowles. Should these
humble lines meet the penetrating and critical
eyes of that gentleman, I should wish him to

know that Mr. Insull of Chicago, Millionaire and Man of Affairs, attributes nine-tenths of all the education he ever had to the versatile and exuberant stream of diverse learning which flowed, long ago, from the tongue of the Editor of *Vanity Fair* to young Insull's pencil.   To-day, Insull is head of all the gas and electric light corporations between Lake Michigan and the Mississippi, as well as of many other gigantic concerns.   Long ago, his business affairs made it necessary that he should become an American citizen, and to that allegiance he has always been loyal, but he has never forgotten his passionate love for the country of his origin, and his pride in the history and achievements of Great Britain is infinite.   For the first two and a half years of war, against many hostile influences, he kept aloft in Chicago the flag of Great Britain.   In private and in public disputation, at bazaars, in Red Cross appeals on behalf of the Allies, his was always the most active and influential voice.   And I think he must have been the happiest man in the United States when at last the country of his origin and the country of his allegiance were ranged side by side as Allies in a common war.

I salute you, Samuel Insull, true and proved

5*

friend of England, across three thousand miles of ocean, and my advice to any Englishman, with claims to know such a man, is that he should not go to Chicago without a letter of introduction to you.

All day long the blizzard blew. From the hotel windows we watched its cruel and devastating violence. I fought my way to the University Club for a Turkish bath, but it took me three quarters of an hour to traverse four blocks back, and twice I was blown over, a humiliated atom, into the snow. No taxis could be obtained. The others stayed in all day.

T. P. O'Connor, who was in Chicago, rang up on the telephone. I was delighted to hear his voice again. I first met him fourteen years ago, when I was his opponent in the Scotland division of Liverpool, and we have always been friends since. He is staying at the Congress Hotel, and I arranged to call and take him to dinner at the Insulls, who have a party for us. But at seven o'clock came a message from our host that it was unsafe for us to venture out. It had taken him an hour to make two miles in his powerful car. More than thirty cars had already been upset by the blizzard and abandoned in snowdrifts until the weather moderated. So we dined quietly at the hotel.

Monday, January 7th.—Yesterday's blizzard had spent, without exhausting, its force, but the whole city wás snow-bound as it has not been within the memory of this generation. Volunteers are called for to clear the streets, which are six feet deep in the drift. The water supplies are threatened and there are ominous whispers that a fire, if it broke out, could have its will of the city. In twenty-four hours eighteen inches of snow had fallen. It is worth while considering, in the light of our worst storms, what such a fall means.

We waded our way for a short distance in the streets and everywhere came across derelict motors. Insull had invited a hundred of the leading citizens of Chicago to meet us at lunch and promised that they should include the most representative men of the City. He certainly was as good as his word. There were present, amongst many others, Judge Alschuler, Judge Baldwin, Judge Brentano, the Attorney-General of Illinois; General Carter, commanding the Central Division of the United States Army; Judge Carter, Judge Carpenter, Mr. Dickinson, once Secretary of State for War; the

President of the National City Bank of Chicago ; Judge Holdon ; Judge Kohlsaat ; Judge O'Connor ; the President of the Continental and Commercial National Bank, and Mr. Shanahan, Speaker of the House of Representatives of the State of Illinois. I spoke for forty-two minutes, and was afterwards, as is the custom, introduced to everybody present.

It was most strongly pressed upon me by those present at the lunch that on my return to Chicago I should address a mass meeting of six thousand, and this I gladly agreed to do. T. P. O'Connor was at the lunch, and came back with me to the hotel for a talk. He is now seventy-one years old, though he has none of the appearance, or manner, or gait, of an old man. His hospitable snuffbox was, as always, ready, though he complained bitterly of the available quality. It seemed to me that it was a fine thing at his age to cross the sea in these dangerous days, and to make himself an exile for so long from all his friends and surroundings. How many men, after passing the allotted span, would be capable of this effort ?

The purpose of his visit to America is to enlist the spirit of Irish-Americans on the side of the Allies, and to convince the American nation that there are sufficient men of different parties in Ireland who believe in that cause to ensure under favourable conditions a majority in the country. I do not know whether he is right or not in this view, but he comes on behalf of John Redmond,* and I wish him well. He has never since his arrival ceased urging the cause of the Allies, as he has constantly urged it in England since August, 1914. We had a long and most friendly talk, both of us hoping that the Irish Convention might arrive at some agreement. I think he has had a hard time in the United States. A section of the Irish-Americans has been most unfriendly to him. Many of his interviews have been misrepresented, so that he had to cease giving them, and he has not thought it wise to hold any public meetings of Irishmen, but he has made many valuable friends, and his tact and persuasiveness have made him the centre in the United States of those many Irishmen who accept the official leadership, and reverence the heroism of Major Willie Redmond.* May he

* These passages were written before the lamented death of Mr. John Redmond.

return safely to Liverpool—*reddas navis incolumem*—with his task accomplished.

Early in the day we had been told it was extremely doubtful whether any train could leave that night for Detroit, but it was finally decided that our train should start at 11.45. We had only two hours to wait at Chicago station, which, under all the conditions, must be accounted satisfactory. But it was most odiously cold. We started at 1.50.

CHAPTER VI

DETROIT AND CLEVELAND—NEW AND KIND
FRIENDS—BACK TO NEW YORK

Tuesday, January 8th.—We arrived at Detroit—a journey of two hundred and eighty-three miles—at 11.15 a.m., but by the Eastern time which prevails, 12.15. We were met by the British Vice-Consul, Mr. E. Meredith, with the disconcerting news that a crowded meeting was waiting for us at 12.30. Travel-stained and weary, we rushed to the Statler Hotel, had the usual "wash and brush up," and then went straight to the meeting. The room held between two and three thousand people, and was crowded to the doors, every gangway being packed by people standing close up to the very edge of the platform. It was exactly the kind of meeting one has on the eve of Polling Day in one's own constituency. I spoke for fifty minutes, and then thought eagerly of a bath and lunch, but the ceremonies were not yet complete. In the same building that well-known and patriotic brotherhood, called the Knights of Columbus, was holding a lunch, consisting of six or seven hundred people. They had urgently pressed their claim to be considered an overflow meeting, and so I went down to their fellowship, and, standing on a table (for there was no other chance of a platform from which to be seen or heard), addressed them for twenty minutes. At the end, those present gave, with startling emphasis, the real American war cry, organized by a " cry conductor," and ended by the audience standing up in a body and singing " God Save the King," the first, though not the last, time I heard it sung by American audiences. It was extremely well sung, with equal harmony and feeling. We were profoundly touched.

The Vice-Consul, Meredith, is a great character, and one of the most attractive and warm-hearted men I have ever met. A Canadian by birth, he has lived for twenty-seven years in the United States, but has never been naturalized. He has a passionate enthusiasm for Great Britain and everything British, and is at the same time extremely popular in the United States. He would sit for hours listening to the stories of British achievements in the war, and asked hundreds of questions as to the conditions in England to-day, and the present spirit of the people. And I remember that when we told him some things about England, the tears rolled silently down his cheek. He was indeed a warm-hearted host, and a noteworthy Briton, whose hand it is good to have clasped in friendship.

He gave us a much-needed lunch at the Detroit Club, and then took us in a car to the Yon de Tega (Town of the Straits Club), a very delightful place. It is, apparently, very exclusive, consisting only of sixty-five members. No name can be proposed for membership except by invitation of the Committee.

He insisted that we should dine with him at the Detroit Club, though by this time, having had little sleep, we could hardly keep our eyes open, and then, on a cold, wet and utterly revolting night, drove us to the railway station, where we entrained for Cleveland. It was hard to leave so friendly a city on so fleeting an acquaintance. I did not see Meredith again before I left the States, but should these lines ever meet his honest eyes, let them convey to him the message that there is a humble house in London which will make him as welcome as he made us in Detroit.

Wednesday, January 9th.—We reached Cleveland at 8 a.m. and were met by Mr. H. H. McKeehan, President of the Cleveland Bar Association, and another Member of the Bar. These gentlemen had been waiting in the cold and draughty station for an hour, as our train was due to arrive at seven. Hospitality, it seems to me, cannot go much further with the temperature at zero.

They took us to the Statler Hotel, and informed us with great delicacy that the Cleveland Bar Association claimed the honour of being our hosts so long as we could stay. A palatial suite of rooms—perhaps the best we have had anywhere—had been reserved. From first to last we were not allowed to spend a penny, or perhaps, in conformity, I ought to say a dime. It is strange how we leave each city greatly grieving over friendships so soon interrupted, and, journeying on, find others equally attractive and warm-hearted. I am sure that this circumstance is a tribute to the change which is taking place all over the States in the feeling towards everything British. The inhabitants of each town welcomed us so warmly because we were representative of a Nation which was now their Ally, of whose alliance they were proud, and on whose stubborn tenacity they greatly relied. Whenever I asked for guidance, whether they would like me to discuss any particular branch of the war, I was over and over again asked to dwell upon the part which Great Britain had played by sea and land, and in the realm of finance. And I never found any audience which did not long to hear of these things, and which was not ready to listen interminably to their explanation.

We were to meet an assembly for luncheon at the large Union Club, and there we found an enormous party, presided over by Colonel Myron T. Herrick, who was the United States Ambassador to France when the war broke out. When the seat of Government was transferred by the French from Paris to Bordeaux, I believe that Herrick was the only Ambassador who remained. He is a very interesting and agreeable man, with an immense admiration for Great Britain and France. The guests at the lunch were very distinguished, consisting of judges, leading lawyers, presidents of banks, and, as we were informed, all the leading business men of the place. Colonel Herrick made a speech introducing us ; I replied, and the Colonel and H. S. were afterwards called upon to speak. Much kindness, humour, and animation.

Mr. McKeehan, who came to meet us in the morning, and is a lawyer in the busiest practice, seems to have devoted his whole time to us, and no one could make acquaintance with Cleveland society of any kind under auspices more tactful or kinder. He presided at 6.30 at one of the largest Bar Association dinners which we had so far attended. I suppose that nearly eight hundred judges and lawyers were met to receive us. Nothing that the most graceful thoughtfulness could conceive was omitted. The menu was beautifully coloured with the linked flags of the United States and Great Britain ; and when I sat down the whole of the meeting stood up and sang every verse of " God Save the King," amid a scene of the most extraordinary enthusiasm. I wished that the King could have heard it. After dinner we had an hour to spare before spending still another night on the train. We saw from the posters that Miss Elsie Janis was appearing in Cleveland that night, and hurriedly extemporized a supper party, almost on our way to the station. The party consisted of Mrs. and Miss Janis, Mr. McKeehan and us three. It was a pleasant end of a very busy day, and the last we saw of McKeehan—the kindest of men—was at 1 a.m. in the morning, waving his hand at that unattractive station,* where he had been waiting for us thirteen hours before. I hope to entertain him one day, even if with rationed hospitality, at Gray's Inn while I am still Treasurer. I can promise him that my fellow benchers will welcome him as warmly as I shall.

Thursday, January 10th.—And so at 6 p.m. we were once again at New York, having completed the first part of our tour. Two other journeys remained. We had just visited the industrial West. We were on the second tour to make the acquaintance of that agricultural West in relation to which it had been ignorantly charged that many farmers did not know that a war was in progress, and that some were even unaware

* I know that I may say this without offence.

of the decease of King George III. It was
felt rightly or wrongly by the Authorities
that a useful work would be done if, on
proper notice, so that the surrounding districts could be present, we addressed a series
of meetings in the capital or important towns
of the agricultural West. In this visit I was
to have the help of American speakers.
And next we had, of course, to visit our
own people in the Dominion of Canada.
We were to leave New York again in two
days, during which time I had four or five
speaking engagements.

But before I attempt to describe any of
these, I propose to lay aside the diary and
discuss in a separate chapter certain points
of importance in relation to the " American
Draft," and amongst them the physique and
morale of the men ; and secondly, certain
other developments which are everywhere
in progress in the Military and Naval progress
of the United States. For a great message
of encouragement is to be drawn from these
efforts. And the encouragement is greater,
not less, when it is remembered—as I hope
may be inferred from my diary—that the
people of the United States are most
assuredly not lagging behind the Govern-

ment. If anything they are ahead of them. Their attitude is not : " Why are the Government committing us so far ? " but, " Why are results so slow ? Why are we not ' mattering ' more now ? "

In the following chapter, therefore, I collect a variety of topics which throw a light upon the character of the American effort. Its position, amid these desultory notes, is open to criticism. But the materials upon which it is based had been collected before I returned to New York ; and I, therefore, put them forward in their chronological order.

CHAPTER VII

THE EFFORT OF THE UNITED STATES

THE most remarkable proof hitherto given by the States of the earnestness with which they entered the war was undoubtedly furnished by the swift adoption of the " Draft " or compulsory service system. It is worth noting that politicians of all schools agree that this step would, at the time it was taken, have been impossible had it not been for our English experience. A very prominent Republican and a Cabinet Minister both concurred in this view. Personally (though I was in France at the time, and all the soldiers were against me*), I always thought that Mr. Asquith's Government was at the outset right in postponing compulsion, at that day, and in the condition in which the Government found itself. I had myself written and spoken in favour of universal military service for many years ; had put it

---

* Poor Neil Primrose and I (a minority of two) had many arguments on this subject at our Headquarters at Hinges.

in all my election addresses in a large working
class constituency ; had successfully, as a
private member, moved the adjournment of
the House to protest against Lord Haldane's
Army reductions in 1906 ; and had received
a copy of Lord Roberts' " Nation in Arms,"
with an inscription thanking me for my
" constant help," but I am none the less of
opinion that, as long as thousands of
volunteers were flocking to the Colours every
day, in numbers so great that it was hopeless
to attempt their equipment for months, the
Radical and Labour Parties would not have
tolerated compulsion. A premature adoption, if I am right in my view, would have
divided the Nation. It is evident that
different considerations arise when one deals
with the period in which the wastefulness
of the voluntary system had become evident,
and its supplies of men were beginning to
dry up. From that time, all my influence,
such as it was, was cast on the side of
compulsion.

It may be incidentally pointed out that
the instantaneous adoption of compulsory
service by the Great Democracy of the West
is a somewhat disconcerting blow to those
who opposed on principle its adoption in

6*

Great Britain. It may, of course, be the fact that the citizens of Great Britain either do possess, or abstractedly ought to possess, rights which no belligerent Government, despotic or democratic, has, in this War, conceded to its own subjects. It may be that, confronted by enemies, all of whom mobilize by force every available individual, and depending upon Allies, some of which have almost sobbed out their man power in the common cause, the citizens of the United Kingdom nevertheless enjoy some unexplained right to immunity from the universal lot of mankind in these bloody days.

It may be so. But the burden of proof would appear to lie upon those who affirm it.

Before the working of the " Draft " is examined, it is right to point out that in America countless numbers of volunteers sprang to the colours long before there was a whisper of compulsion. And if compulsion had been withheld, it is not unreasonable to suppose that the volunteer effort of the States might even have equalled that of the British Empire. And in acceding to this view I make, for an Englishman, a very great admission. A striking feature of the pre-draft days was the number of young American gentlemen who hastened to enlist as privates. The Philadelphia City Troop, formerly the Bodyguard of Washington, is the oldest military organization in the United States. It is composed of the sons of local gentlemen, and its members volunteered to a man as private soldiers. They were afterwards, as was the case with our Public School Battalion, used as material for the Officers' Training Schools, but the example, none the less, was offered.

Squadron A of New York is a similar organization, half club, half military unit. It prides itself, justly, upon the same hereditary *esprit de corps*. Its members are almost all representative business men in New York. It is an old association possessing, as does the Philadelphia City Troop, a distinguished record of active service. Here, too, the members volunteered to a man as private soldiers.

These two associations are representative and many others could be cited.

Perhaps even more striking is the list of men of great rank or possessions who, instead

of going away sorrowful, immediately enlisted in the ranks. Amongst these may be
mentioned Joseph Daniels, Junior, son of Mr.
Secretary Daniels, who joined the Marine
Corps; Humphrey Redfield, son of the
Minister of Commerce, who enlisted as an
ordinary rating in the Navy; Secretary
Houston's son, who did the same. But the
list could be made indefinitely long. Two
sons of Secretary Wilson joined the Army as
privates, so did Franklin Lane, Junior, a
son of Secretary Lane, though he has since
received a commission. Charlie Taft, the
son of ex-President Taft, is to-day a sergeant
in the Army. Francis Roche, a grandson of
Frank Roche, the millionaire, became an
ordinary rating, as did Paul Warburg, whose
father is many times a millionaire and a
member of the Federal Reserve Board.
Edwin Denby is forty years old, President of
the Denby Motor Trust, President of the
Board of Commerce, and for two years a
Member of Congress. He enlisted as a
private in the Marine Corps. Marshall Field,
who, I am told, is worth roughly eighty
million dollars, is to-day a private in the
National Army, and I have already given the
instance of Mitchell, the ex-Mayor of New

York, who served as a private soldier at Plattsburg, and has since, at the age of forty-two, received a commission as major in the military service of the country.

I cannot pass from this topic without a reference to the family of that fine veteran, Lieut.-General Sam Young, who entered the Civil War as a private in a cavalry regiment and returned as the commanding officer of the entire American Army. In this war he has four sons-in-law and five grandsons engaged, one of the grandsons, not yet eighteen years old, being a sergeant of cavalry, as his grandfather was over half a century ago. Surely a fine type of American family !

These instances, selected almost at random, illustrate the spirit and gallantry with which the better known families, socially and politically, have thrown themselves into the war.

But no reflection can properly be made upon those who waited for the draft, for it became known almost from the outset that the draft was coming. And when it came, it worked with an almost incredible smoothness. Conscientious objectors have been few, perhaps because they were not given quite the suggestive encouragement of the special clause in our Act. I may make this criticism of our method inasmuch as I was one who helped to draft it. The difficulties at that moment seemed to us greater than, in the event, they proved.

From the start the classes answered to the call in almost exactly the same numbers as were anticipated. Some forty great camps were formed in different parts of the country, containing on the average thirty or thirty-five thousand men. The camps sprang up with almost incredible swiftness. They required for their construction 100,000,000 feet of timber; 100,000 car-loads of material were absorbed in their supply. The labour of more than 100,000 manual labourers was constantly bestowed upon them, until the moment of their completion. No sooner were their new homes ready than 1,500,000 soldiers in the making swarmed down upon them like locusts. For days the railways did little but military transport work. And not one life was lost in the process.

The States, like Great Britain, deprived themselves, for a great end, of the immense usefulness of their regular army for purposes of instruction, and were driven to improvise their new armies with the aid of such instructors as were left, reinforced by those gladly lent by France and Great Britain. The task of training such enormous numbers of young men was stupendous. It was only rendered possible by the patience and the unremitting industry of the instructors, and by the superb quality of the raw material. I have never in my life seen finer young men than those who in these distant camps are to-day acquiring the military art. Broad-shouldered, athletic, clean-limbed, bright-complexioned, in the very flower of youth, they may be matched in physique with any soldiers who, from any country, have offered their lives to the desperate hazards of this war. And their earnestness in the business is quite extra-ordinarily impressive. The ship which carries me to England contains thousands of men and hundreds of officers. The O.C. troops on board on the first morning summoned all the officers into the reading-room, and made them a most admirable, manly and soldierly address, informing them in detail of the duties expected of them while on board. He concluded with equal dignity and good sense, " Remember this above all, you are not on an American ship. Many who watch your conduct, however friendly they may be, will be busy to note how the members of a new army demean themselves. See to it that your conduct be worthy of the military traditions of our past, and of the high expectations with which your country has sent you forth." Those whom he addressed listened to him, standing in respectful and disciplined attention, as I have seen British officers listen to a general of distinguished rank. Since the ship started no American officer has gambled, and none (unless in disregard of orders) has tasted alcohol. And all day long, the decks of the ship resound with the tread of men undergoing either drill or physical exercise. In the evening staff officers or others are busy with lectures, and at spare moments during the day dozens of young Americans can be seen engaged with French grammars or dictionaries. It is a very earnest Army, very like the First Hundred Thousand, and I discern nowhere, in any rank, any assertiveness or unsoldierly quality.

From the start, the orders of the day in camp showed how much was expected of the new American Army. The following was

given to me at one of the camps as the daily
schedule of work :

6.30 ....Breakfast.
7.30 to 8.0........Physical exercise.
8.0 to 9.0.........Bayonet combat.
9.0 to 9.30........Bombing.
9.30 to 10.0.......Musketry or light machine-gun
                    practice.
10.0 to 12.0.......Close order training.
12.0 ....Dinner.
1.30 to 4.30.......Practice marches, tactical
                    problems, scouting, patrolling.
5.15 ....Supper.
5.45 ....Retreat.

And this programme is without prejudice
to the daily routine of schools and conferences, at which the attendance of officers
and non-commissioned officers is required.
Secretary Baker informed the Committee of
the Senate that there are at present in France
more than two hundred thousand American
soldiers, that by the spring of this year there
will be five hundred thousand, and that before
1918 is over one million five hundred thousand will be ready for service overseas.
The first figure is already realized ; Secretary
Daniels has guaranteed that, with the help
of the Allies, the second will be attained, and

it may be assumed that the third will either altogether, or approximately, be realized. It is, therefore, and it ought to be, a source of most profound encouragement to the war-worn troops of France and Great Britain that these unlimited numbers of superb young men, seriously and most carefully trained, are available as an inexhaustible reservoir of man power. And we should never forget that it is a demonstrable historical truth that in the qualities of soldierly value, unless the stock has been impaired by alien infiltrations, nations, when tested to their core, invariably revert to type. The young men who are marching with high heads to range themselves by the side of our veterans are the descendants of those who conquered at Gettysburg, who died at Antietam, and who resisted, till all was lost, the bloody assaults of the Wilderness.

But the prospect of using these great resources depends once again upon the question of tonnage. If the ships can be found to bring over to Europe these highly trained young men, largely the same superb stock as our own Canadian soldiers, they will be available in unfailing numbers every month and every year, till the day comes when a decisive result in the West is certain.

No doubt mistakes have been made in the United States, just as they were made in Great Britain and elsewhere. No doubt a hundred points of legitimate criticism may be made. It is not wise either to ignore American mistakes or to exaggerate British mistakes. But the moral grandeur of the decision—the stupendous decision—taken by the United States will last as long as the history of great nations is the subject-matter of chronicle. For this country has, deliberately and with full knowledge, determined to make an immense military contribution to the armies of Europe, three or four thousand miles away from its base, across an ocean infested by submarines, at a time when it had to improvise armies, to provide all their military equipment, to manufacture no small part of the necessary tonnage, and to supply and finance many of the Allies. The voice of criticism may well be silent in the face of a resolution so sublime. No nation in the world has ever proposed to itself such a task. No nation in the world but the United States could accomplish it. I am certain that they can and that they will.

The statesmen of Germany staked all they had in the belief that they could not or would not.

Let me quote in this connection the resolute statement which Mr. Secretary Baker, formerly, as we have seen, an earnest pacifist, made before the Committee of the Senate :

" Our enemy is on the other side of a mighty ocean. Our problem is to cross it and reach him. We have made an immense effort to meet an immense obligation. Very soon we shall demonstrate upon the battle-fields of Europe our determination to win the war. The day is now very close when we shall strike, and strike worthily of those who went before us."

The part played by the United States Navy, though less spectacular, has been little less remarkable.

When America entered the war, the chief question engaging the attention of sailors was, of course, the submarine menace. The chief subjects of American maritime policy were :

1. The offensive against submarines ;

2. The transport of American troops and supplies to France, a topic naturally including the larger question of tonnage.

1. *Submarines*. The ingenuity of American Naval designers and constructors has long been well known, and the service threw itself with characteristic energy into the task of grappling with the pest, whose destruction or control is necessary if the armies of the United States are to exercise a decisive influence in Europe. An initial programme was immediately adopted and as its general features have been made public by the authorities, I may summarize them without indiscretion. Mr. Secretary Daniels, like Mr. Secretary Baker, believes "that it is more important to keep the people of this country informed of the progress of war preparations than to attempt, with very doubtful results, to mystify the enemy." The programme, then, which is now being carried out comprises in the first place the building of two hundred and sixty destroyers. As soon as it is possible this number will be increased, and it will constantly be developed until the task is accomplished.

Our Allies (if I may loosely call them so) are building three hundred and fifty smaller vessels of a type known as submarine chasers. These will be 110 feet long, possessing a speed of sixteen or seventeen knots, and built of wood. They will be extremely seaworthy, and will cross the Atlantic Ocean under their own power. They were laid down in order to utilize that part of the country's building facilities which were not suitable for the construction of larger merchant ships, whether of steel or wood.

More than one hundred submarines are at this moment under construction. This work is being pressed forward with the utmost possible expedition and concentration. All of these, as and when finished, either have been, or will be sent, to bases in European waters. The American Naval Air Service is already co-operating vigorously in coastal operations against submarines. An immense amount of additional material will soon be available in this connection. Finally, though here I am bound to be very reticent, a large number of great and promising undertakings, to deal with the submarine menace, are well advanced already. These are of too secret a nature to be divulged. Some are offensive, some are defensive in their character. They are stamped with all the qualities which we have learned to associate with American ingenuity.

2. *Transport of Troops to France.* Very little has been published by authority on this subject, except that all German ships in American ports, amounting to seven hundred and fifty thousand tons, including the *Vaterland* and the *Kronprinzessin Cecelie*, were taken over by the Government. The declared policy of the Government is that all ships employed in Army service shall be manned by the Navy, and the crews consequently are subject to naval discipline, and practically all these ships are already so manned. This necessitated an expansion of naval personnel from sixty thousand to one hundred and fifty thousand regulars, and, in addition, sixty thousand naval reserves, which, as an initial step, has been done. The American Navy, with such British assistance as is available, now undertakes, and will continue to undertake, almost the entire convoy and protection of American troops overseas. Every American merchant ship either has been or will be armed. All clearing for war zones are powerfully armed, and the guns are manned by fully trained naval ratings.

7

The building of merchant ships is, of course, not primarily a naval matter. It is under the United States Shipping Board (the Emergency Fleet Corporation). This is a private concern in which the Government owns one hundred per cent. of the stock, and thus takes all the risk. Before the United States of America came into the war seven hundred and fifty million dollars were appropriated to build ships. A further appropriation of seven hundred and fifty million dollars has been submitted to the present session of Congress in order to continue the work.

Fifty-two yards have been largely expanded to provide facilities for building. In addition, seventy-four more new yards have been started. Of these last, three will be the largest in the world. Each yard will have from twenty to fifty structural steel shops working for it at various places. Many figures have been quoted as to the estimated output, but no official estimate has been published for this or succeeding years. The premature announcement of inflated estimates can do nothing but harm. This much, however, can be said; the realized output of merchant ships for 1918 will be greatly in excess of the greatest output of merchant ships by Great Britain in any year previous to the war. And the United States of America have not, since the Civil War, been a shipbuilding nation.

A word may be added in reference to the preparations now being made in the States for the war in the air. Exact predictions defining the contribution of the United States in aeroplanes may prove to be very disappointing, and I find those who were in the best position to judge very cautious in putting forward estimates. It was pointed out by high authority that no particularly useful purpose was served by announcing programmes, the realization of which was uncertain. Such a course may terrify the enemy into exertions which he could not otherwise make, and may possibly unduly reassure the Allies, and so render them less enterprising.

But while observing this caution, it may be stated that well-informed persons have no doubt that from the 1st of June, 1918, to the 1st of June, 1919, the United States will be able to supply one hundred thousand Liberty engines.

It is not claimed for the Liberty engine that it is a new American invention. A

7*

committee of the most able experts in the United States met to consider the engine question, and eventually all the best points of all the most efficient existing engines were, in the opinion of those consulted, collected in the Liberty engine. It is not claimed that it is yet perfect, but it has sustained a test of fifty-three hours' run in the shops, and has given every satisfaction when flown in the air. A remarkable feature in the engine is that its adaptors have succeeded in reducing the weight from two and a quarter lbs. per horse power to one and nine-tenths lbs. per horse power.

It is not anticipated that the supply of aeroplanes in the United States will keep pace with the supply of the engines. But the raw material will be forthcoming, and there is no reason why the actual planes should not be readily manufactured in Europe.

It is not necessary to say much about the aviation schools now in existence, or in process of formation. They are being organized with the science and thoroughness which one expects from Americans in such matters, and the native audacity of the American youth, together with his mechanical skill and ingenuity, should make him an ideal pilot, worthy to take his place side by side with the d'Artagnans of the air who have brought such immortal glory to the martial annals of France and Great Britain.

I cannot in this connection resist telling an anecdote which throws a light upon the sources recruiting that ever glorious Lafayette Squadron, which gallant American boys contributed to the French Army while the States were still neutral.

I remember in 1912, while on a visit to Newport, going to a fancy dress ball given by Mrs. Cornelius Vanderbilt, Junior. It did not end till daybreak. And a controversy arose between poor Edward Horner and myself on the one hand, and two American young men on the other, as to whether or not we could beat them at lawn tennis. We were at the moment supping (or breakfasting) together.

We decided to adjourn to a neighbouring court and determine the wager which was proposed. A young boy (perhaps sixteen years old) offered to umpire and mounted the high umpire stand. The result of the game does not matter. But, in the excitement, the spectators, who were numerous—and all in fancy dress—pressed upon the umpire's box, and upset it, with the result that the umpire broke his ankle.

Four years later I was lunching at the Ritz Hotel, Paris, and was introduced to a soldierly young man in the uniform of a sergeant in the French Flying Corps. " Are you," he asked me, " the F. E. Smith who played a tennis match at 5 a.m. at Newport in 1912 ? " I answered " Yes." " Do you remember the umpire who broke his ankle ? " " Yes." " I was that umpire." And this boy had been flying for a year as a non-commissioned officer in the armies of France.

All honour to him, and to the valiant squadron of which he was a member ! It is now reunited to its own armies. May its future be worthy of its glorious past !

A final and very short word may be added on the subject of finance. Everybody in Europe knows almost with precision the stupendous results of the Liberty Loans. The financial outcome of the great oratorical campaign, which preceded the issue, was hardly more important than the great work of influencing opinion, which was achieved by the speeches made all over the States to support it, but on its purely financial side the result was amazing and incalculable.

Most people know, too, in general, the extraordinarily lavish contributions which the United States have made to those who are distressed among her new confederates. I do not know what is the staggering total of all the amounts which Congress has appropriated to the purposes of the war. But I saw it stated in a financial journal of repute that if one took two columns, and placed in one all the billions of dollars which previous Senates had voted for public purposes from the date of the Declaration of Independence to August, 1914, and then placed in an opposite column all that Congress had voted from August, 1914, to January, 1917, the first claim would only exceed the record by some seven billions of dollars. I cannot vouch for the figures, but I was told by a very experienced financier that there was nothing at all incredible in them. In relation to the totals in each column, the difference is, of course, insignificant, and it has now probably disappeared altogether.

I have only a word to add. I have attempted in this chapter, in the most general manner, to describe the gigantic exertions of all kinds which this strong, generous and inexhaustible Nation is making and contemplating. If there are any who, amid the horrors of this long-drawn struggle, tend to lose heart, let them look upon all this achievement, actual and future, and remember that they are confronted with only two alternatives at this moment. The first is to accept an inglorious peace, acknowledging that all those bitter sacrifices have been made in vain; that the gallant dead have spent their lives without avail, and that the goal is too difficult for the countrymen of Chatham to attain. The second is to stand stubbornly and tenaciously where they have held the line since August, 1914; strong and fearless in the certainty that if they will hold out till America finds her strength, the end of this struggle is as certain as it is certain that the dawn follows the night. And the end is that the Anglo-Saxon nations of the world, in perpetual comradeship with their war-tried Latin comrades in Italy and France, will maintain through the ages the peace of the World and the sanctity of Public Law.

> " O well for him whose will is strong!
> He suffers, but he will not suffer long."

CHAPTER VIII

WE were seven hours late when our train
drew in at the station at 6.15 p.m. We
had met at Washington, R. W. Goelet
(better known as Bertie, to distinguish him
from his cousin, whose name and initials
are the same). He had most hospitably
invited us to stay with him at his beautiful
house, 591 Fifth Avenue, on any future
visits to New York. And henceforward his
house was our headquarters. He was
indeed a genial and perfect host. We did
what we liked; came in when we liked;
went out when we liked. If we wanted to
have meals at his house, they were ready;
if not, no questions were asked. Our host
was out when we arrived, and we dined
quietly the first night with Colonel Riggs,
a friend of his, who has been doing Red

Cross work in France since the commence-
ment of the war, and is about to return for
the third time.

Friday, January 11th.—To-night is the
annual meeting of the New York Bar Association, presided over by Judge Hughes, who
was the Republican candidate at the last
Presidential election and formerly a most
distinguished member of the Supreme Court.
I had been invited when in England to deliver
the annual address, and had given as much
thought to it as circumstances allowed since
I left London.   After considerable discussion
with Judge Hughes and with Judge Wadhams,
the Secretary of the Association, I had decided
while passing through New York, on my first
visit, to give it the title, " LAW, WAR and
the FUTURE."   It had been suggested that
I should speak on the League of Nations ;
but I preferred to select a title which gave
me a wider range.   It was specially asked
that I should speak only on some subject
which related to the war.

I was much interested in meeting Judge
Wadhams, because of his name.   Twenty-
seven years ago I became a scholar of
Wadham College, Oxford, and I owe to

that foundation such academic success as I gained at Oxford, and much of any success which I have met with since. I am to-day an honorary fellow of the College. I suspected that a name so uncommon must be drawn from that sturdy and public-spirited Somersetshire Knight, whose noble gift to learning is commemorated by the most beautiful and symmetrical building in Oxford. Nor was I wrong. The Judge had satisfied himself that his family was descended from the same fine old stock, and gave me an explanation of the superfluous " s " in his name, which I think followed the analogy of the final " s " in Jones.

I ought to explain that the annual meeting of the Bar of New York is attended almost as a ritual by all the lawyers of consequence in this great city. It is certainly a very able, and a very critical audience.

Judge Hughes gave a large dinner before the meeting, consisting of some sixty or seventy guests of both sexes. After the dinner we adjourned to a large public hall with galleries, in which the members of the Association and their ladies collected. It was very crowded. Perhaps seventeen hundred people in all.

I attempted first an analysis of the elements involved in the conception of Law, distinguishing, as far as I could, its scientific from its metaphorical uses. There was, of course, nothing new in this to those who are familiar with the writings of Austin, Bentham, Maine and Holland. I then examined the conception and the definition of International Law. I attempted a short historical estimate of the labours of Ayala and Grotius. I drew the obvious distinctions between Private Law and Public Law, and dwelt for a moment in passing upon the commonplace, that, until the sanctions of International Law are, in some way or other, reinforced so as to gain a force comparable to the sanctions of Private Law, there is security in the world neither for civilization nor Christianity.

This brought me by a natural transition to President Wilson's noble and most eloquently-expressed conception of that League of Nations, which is relied upon to safeguard the future of the world. It did not appear to me worthy of the quality of the audience I was addressing, and certainly not of the high office which I hold, that I should spend what remained of my allotted hour in merely rhetorical commendations of an ideal, which has no value whatever unless it can be brought into conformity with the realities of life, with what, for want of a better term, may be called the biological tendencies of the human race. And these tendencies, it is evident, must be examined over a period sufficiently long to afford the material for a generalization. Prefacing, therefore, my analysis with the statement that the task indicated by the President deserved and required the zealous co-operation of all men of good will, and constructive resource, in the Allied countries, I devoted myself to the task of examining some of the difficulties which the world had to face before this ideal could be realized. The essence of the proposal is a league of nations pledged (and strong enough) to compel by force the obedience of a recalcitrant member to the collective decision. If this condition cannot be secured, the whole scheme is futile and foredoomed to failure. Many difficulties emerge at once. Are the Central Powers, on the conclusion of the war, to be admitted, and if so, when, to such a league ?

The answer to this question would appear to depend, first, upon the completeness of the victory over them, and, secondly, upon the form of the constitutions under which they respectively emerge from the war. A second necessary condition would appear to be that the league should reach agreement as to the military establishments which each of its members should be allowed to maintain. The obstacles in the way of such agreement are patent, and need not be elaborated. A public discussion of them, such as is apparently contemplated, hardly lessens the evident difficulty. And a further question arises, whether any, and what, special arrangement, would be required in the case of an insular Power, possessing no army, and relying for its protection upon maritime and air defence ? It seemed to me not altogether unreasonable that an Englishman should suggest this difficulty. A third and more fundamental consideration arises when one attempts to think out the functions of such a league, in relation to those inevitable changes which the evolution of humanity brings to the relative strength of Nations.

I indicated these and a number of less obvious difficulties, suggesting when I could (which was not always) an answer, partial or complete, but always in the spirit of sympathy, and always insisting that the league could never be realized unless the difficulties were boldly and clearly faced, so that those who come together when these unhappy days are ended, to give it form and shape, may have the best answer available to difficulties which are certain to be most insistently pressed.

The address, though technical and not in the least rhetorical, was well received. And although a few papers superficially miscon-strued it as lacking in sympathy for the President's proposals, nearly all of the better-known papers recognized it as a contribution which, though analytic and critical, was intended to be, and was, in fact, helpful.*

After the meeting came a reception in which I was introduced to many of those present. And then home, where we saw the end of a small but very pleasant dance which Goelet was giving at his home. To bed about three o'clock, after an interesting and varied evening.

Saturday, January 12th.—I had an engage-ment to lunch at one o'clock " down-town "

---

* I have unexpectedly received the transcript of this address and publish it, with none but verbal alterations, in the following chapter.

at the Lawyers' Club. The Colonel went with me. There were also present the Italian Ambassador and the Belgian Minister. It is a very important club, with spacious and even splendid rooms, I believe—I cannot precisely remember—about twenty stories high. I remember that it was sufficiently high to justify a " non-stop elevator." The large room was crowded, even uncomfortably so. I suppose there were five hundred people present. The Chairman proposed the health of the guests. My Italian and Belgian colleagues asked me to reply on their behalf and my own, which I did in a speech of thirty-five minutes. At the end of the proceedings the Committee elected us, all three, life members of the Club, with all the privileges of full membership. So that, when I return to New York, I shall always have a club " down-town " at which I can entertain my friends. This greatly pleased me, for, as I have said, Wall Street has always terrified me. Now, I have a home there.

The dinner of the Ohio Society of New York, under the presidency of Colonel Myron Herrick—of whom I have already spoken —was to take place at 7.30, at the Waldorf-Astoria Hotel. Here Colonel Roose-

velt and myself were to be the speakers. It
was one of the principal engagements I had
come from England to keep, and the organi-
zers had very courteously put my name down
as the first speaker. But I felt that the
Colonel was a man of world-wide distinction.
He had been twice President of the United
States. He had been the friend of kings and
the adviser of emperors. I had never heard
him speak on an important occasion. Some
twelve hundred guests of the highest distinction were present at this most brilliant
function, and I thought I should like to
hear him speak before the audience was
weary. I asked him how long he thought he
would be, to which he replied, about thirty
minutes. He very kindly undertook to
speak first, by which decision, to tell the
truth, I was much relieved, for I had already
made ten times as many speeches as I liked,
and most of them had been widely reported.
In fact, the Colonel spoke with great vigour
and picturesqueness for an hour and a
quarter, of which I did not grudge him a
moment, and indeed everyone knows the
difficulty of an estimate in these matters.
His speech consisted mainly of criticisms
upon the administration, on the ground that

8

they were not " speeding up " the war fast
enough.   He developed his criticisms in
detail, and with his well-known vigour and
humour.   I was naturally unable to form,
and still less to express, any judgment upon
most of the points raised by him, but I remember he said, with great effect, after calling
attention to the case of a battalion which,
after many months, according to the speaker,
possessed neither rifles nor machine-guns :
" I shall be told that I am giving information
to the Germans.   Don't you believe it.   The
Germans know already.   And if they don't
know already, what are the Bulgarian and
Turkish embassies for ? "

This thrust aroused great merriment, and,
indeed, the whole of his trenchant speech
was very loudly cheered.   Another reference
to the refusal of the administration to accept
his military services suggested an amusing
passage.   Commenting on what he alleged
to be dilatory in the preparations of the
Government, he pointed to the speed with
which he had raised, equipped and trained a
regiment in the Spanish War.   " For I was
in that war, but that was a less exclusive
war."   The word " exclusive " with a drawl
characteristic of the ex-President, when he

wishes to produce one of his sarcastic effects.

And in a more serious vein to which the audience, in a swift change from satire to gravity, adapted itself, as only an American audience can : " Never forget that this fight is primarily, and not only secondarily, America's fight. Our troops fight abroad beside their allies to-day in order that to-morrow they may not fight without allies beside their ruined homes."

This serious and (it seemed to me) true warning was received with earnest expressions of agreement.

I did not get up to speak until eleven o'clock, but was told it was essential I should speak until 11.30, as the audience certainly would not be content with less. I attempted to compress within this period a compendious, but still, I hope, a moderately complete summary of what Great Britain and the Empire have done and suffered in the war. It was received, as everything one says to these warm-hearted people is received, with the greatest kindness and sympathy.

There was taking place this same night the annual banquet of the New York Bar Association, which is always held on the night after the annual meeting. I had promised to go on and say a few words at this dinner. I got there at 11.45. It was, however, still proceeding with unabated vigour, the members and their guests being as numerous as at the other banquet. Judge Hughes was in the chair ; His Excellency, the Governor-General of Canada, the Duke of Devonshire, was one of the guests, and I was told on my arrival that he had delivered an earnest and weighty speech. And when I entered the room, Elihu Root was ending what seemed to be a most eloquent and moving address. They called on me to speak, and, as the phrase goes, I said a few words, only taking ten minutes.

On this night—such were the hectic conditions of our tour—we were due to take the train to start on our second venture, which was to make Chicago the base. Ben Ali Haggin, the artist, of whom I have already spoken, had invited us on our way from these banquets to the early morning train—which left at 4.30—to sup in his studio. We found a most delightful party, consisting of about forty people. Hartley Manners, Miss Maxine Elliott, Miss Laurette Taylor, Miss

Ethel Barrymore, Miss Lyn Fontanne, and
a large number of men whom we knew,
including the Duke's aides-de-camp. We
left (reluctantly and prematurely) about
4 a.m., crossed the river in a most intense
cold (ten degrees below zero), and boarded
the car at 5.15. We were to sleep in it for
eight successive nights, making speeches
every day.

CHAPTER IX

PROCEEDINGS OF THE NEW YORK STATE BAR
ASSOCIATION ON FRIDAY EVENING,
JANUARY 11TH, 1918.

PRESIDENT CHARLES E. HUGHES, Presiding.

PRESIDENT HUGHES: Gentlemen of the
Bar Association, Ladies and Gentlemen. It
has been our good fortune in the years gone
by to welcome many of our brethren of the
Bar from the other side of the sea—lawyers
of Great Britain, lawyers of France, lawyers
of Italy. We have had frequent occasion
in welcoming those from Great Britain and
the Dominion of Canada to speak of the fact
that political separation did not result in
the severance of those ties made by language
and tradition and the common service of
the system of jurisprudence, which has given
us the same ideals of liberty under law.

But to-night the occasion is one of peculiar interest. We welcome to-night a distinguished member of the Bar of Great Britain, the head of the Bar of Great Britain, not to speak of the traditions which we have held in common, not to speak of the common source of our common jurisprudence and of the great names in the law who have furnished us with our professional ideals—we remember all that—we emphasize that; but the meeting to-night has a far deeper significance. We are here to-night not to remember so much what has united us in the past, but to remember what it is that we unitedly oppose at the present. (Applause.) We are here with the representatives of our Allies (Applause)—the representative of His Majesty the King of Italy (Applause); the representative of His Majesty the King of England, the Governor-General of Canada (Applause); and with our brother in the law, and our brother in arms, the representative of a fighting lawyer—first in war, first in peace, and first in the hearts of all true-hearted Britons and Americans.

I introduce Sir Frederick Smith, the Attorney-General of Great Britain. (Prolonged applause.)

ADDRESS OF SIR FREDERICK SMITH.

SIR FREDERICK SMITH: Mr. Justice
Hughes, my Brethren of the Bar of the
State of New York. Many distinguished
predecessors, either holding my position in
the Bar of Great Britain, or high judicial
position, have had the honour of addressing
their Brethren of the Bar of the State of
New York. They have done so under circumstances more favourable, because more
leisurely, than those conceded to me. They
have, therefore, been able to lend to their
observations a literary atmosphere worthy
of the audiences which they have addressed.

I, Mr. Justice Hughes, address you under
the least auspicious circumstances that can
be conceived. Since I first landed in your
country a fortnight ago, I have travelled
many, many thousands of miles; I have
spent the last four nights in your hospitable
railway trains, under circumstances, I believe,
in which they have not done themselves
full justice (Laughter); I have made, I
suppose, in the last fortnight or three weeks,
as many as twenty or thirty speeches; and
under those circumstances you will not, I
know, exact from me the same finish or per-

fection of form which the Bar of New York
has been accustomed to claim from the Bar
of England.   But you will accept the will, in
substitute for the performance, as an indication of what I should have attempted had I addressed you under more normal circumstances.

Mr. Justice Hughes, no English lawyer can
ever feel anything but at home when he
addresses American lawyers.   The reasons
are, indeed, simple.   The mighty streams of
Anglo-Saxon jurisprudence spring, after all,
from a common source, and no circumstance
is more commonly reflected upon with pride
by English lawyers, than that the constitutions of all your States, but two, contain a
reservation to the effect that where no other
law applies, the doctrine and the conclusions
of the English common law shall determine
controversies within their confines.   I may,
perhaps, cite a further illustration, drawn
from my own experience : It has been my
fortune, as law adviser of the British Government in the last three years, to argue many
cases in our Prize Courts.   In the earliest
stages of those arguments, I was conscious
of some embarrassment, if and when I reflected upon the view which was held of them
by some American lawyers.   But I assure

you that no authorities were more frequently cited by me before the President of our Prize Court, Sir Samuel Evans, and before the Privy Council, which is our Appellate Court on prize matters, than those decisions of your great American judges which are contained in the reports of Wallace and Cranch. I am sure that American lawyers would have been proud if they could have observed, as I have done (sometimes to my confusion as an advocate), the respect which is daily paid in the highest courts in our country to the judgments of the distinguished judges whose decisions are recorded in those historical reports.

Mr. Chairman, at first sight superficial persons may be tempted to the conclusion that this is not a war which very much concerns lawyers. I take a different view. I think that it is a war, of all the wars which have ever been waged, that concerns lawyers, because it is more directly and more demonstrably related to legal problems than any of the great wars of the world.

I have chosen to-night a wide subject, one which enables me, with your kind indulgence, to touch, with superficial treatment, upon a variety of subjects. The title of the address to which you are good enough to listen is, "Law, War and the Future." I and those who listen to me are supposed to be learned in the law. In the language of Horace, we are *legum jurisque periti*, but, with the skill of our science, we have, I believe, fastened upon the laymen of this country and our own a higher degree of responsibility than we have ever accepted in our own case, because every layman in our country, and I suspect every layman in this country, is bound at his peril to understand the law; but as I understand your law and ours, we lawyers can only be called upon for a reasonable understanding of the law. (Laughter.) Most of us are busy practitioners, and we give advice to people who find themselves in difficulties in the affairs of daily life. I suspect that in the stress of practice we may forget those far-away student days, when we brooded under compulsion over the philosophical but somewhat arid volumes of Austin. I doubt whether there is a practitioner at the Bar listening to me to-day who, in his younger days, was not compelled, or, at any rate, exhorted, to study the volumes of this sound, but unsensational, Apostle of Analysis. (Laughter.)

Well, sir, I hope that you have maintained in its unimpaired integrity the fresh and fragrant impressions which I, and no doubt you, in youth derived from those volumes. (Laughter.) I am about to ask you (making a great strain upon your friendly indulgence) to recall what has been the conception of law, not as we have occasion to realize it in our daily practice, but as it was analysed for us in our youth by the great writers who have become classical names in the history of jurisprudence.

I suppose that, in its proper sense, law is adequately defined as an instruction, or a prohibition, issuing from an organized and sovereign society, to persons within the jurisdiction, and fortified by an appropriate sanction. There are many uses of the term " law " which are analogous or purely metaphorical, which writers who have dwelt upon the inevitableness of law—upon the familiar experience that when the law issues certain injunctions or prescriptions certain consequences follow—have invented by way of metaphor. Instances of such metaphorical use can be found in the phrases : " The law of gravity," or " the law of refraction." A well-known writer* has pointed out how

* My old teacher and friend, Sir T. E. Holland.

merely metaphorical such terms are in relation to the severe and proper conception of the term *law*. When you say there is a law of gravity or a law of refraction, all you mean is that under certain physical conditions objects are refracted or objects do gravitate. But, sir, these uses of the term "law" are of very small importance in relation to the use of the term "law" which a lawyer, addressing lawyers, is bound to make. I am chiefly concerned to-night, attempting as I am to develop the conception of law in its relation to the great world crisis in which we find ourselves, to lay stress upon the coercive element in the conception of law, the sanction which visits with punitive consequences the citizen who is in breach of the law.

Sir, in our domestic law, the power of punishing the man who is in breach of the law is essential to its very conception. No state is civilized which has not, in the first place, this conception of law, and which does not, in the second, associate in its execution the consequence, that any man who breaks the law suffers; he is chastised by Authority. And if you ask an educated citizen which of all the elements in law is the most characteristic, he will undoubtedly reply that it is to be found in the fact that the man who disobeys the law sustains punishment at the hands of Society. I merely restate this commonplace and familiar doctrine because I invite you next, by way of contrast, to consider the conception of International Law. Then I shall ask you to allow me to develop some general observations upon the elements of resemblance and the elements of distinction between the two.

An adequate definition for our purpose of International Law is, perhaps—the body of doctrine which civilized nations have agreed to accept among themselves as binding with a degree of obligation comparable to that which they concede to their own municipal laws.* Let me, if you will allow me—because in a matter which is historically so obscure one can only proceed by a series of guesses —let me attempt, in the most superficial way, to trace the probable origin of International Law, or the public law of states. The subject is unfamiliar to the ordinary practitioner, for although you are in your practices familiar with what is sometimes

* This is, roughly, Hall's definition.

called under a misleading label, " Private International Law," there are probably not many among you who have been called upon to consider, or to conduct cases, which fall under the head of Public International Law.

The development of this doctrine from the earliest days of civilization has been slow, painful and laborious. It probably sprang in the very infancy of humanity from the concessions which were made to heralds ; from the immunity, gradually established, which conceded to heralds some degree of protection ; for it is obvious that if heralds had not been protected from violence the career of a herald would gradually have ceased to attract (Laughter) ; and, therefore, in elementary communities international intercourse would have been difficult, if not impossible. You will remember that in the Old Testament, when the ambassadors of David were sent back with one side of their beards shaved off, it was generally felt that the matter had been carried too far. (Loud laughter.) But, Sir, we must pass over, with hurried and superficial survey, centuries of human life, recording merely the conclusion that there has hardly been a nation, there has hardly been even a tribe, in the world's history, so uncivilized as not to recognize that there must be some channel, protected from violence, through which the public communications of one community might be conveyed to the authorities of another community. So if you take the *jus fetiale* of Rome, you may find the cradle in which International Law had its germinal growth. But many bitter, bloody centuries were to pass over the world before even the infancy of that science, as we understand it to-day, was safely traversed. The mediæval world passed through a welter of unredeemed savagery. Almost a hundred and forty years of strife convulsed the Continent of Europe, during which men knew no public law, during which the license of soldiers was controlled by no legal proscription, before we come to that memorable century in which the humane and versatile genius of Grotius first began to collect the elemental sources from which International Law ultimately rose.

I ask you to consider at the outset of this branch of my address how vital it is to civilization and to humanity that there should exist some system of public law able to command the obedience of the civilized world.

I have attempted to analyse the qualities which, of all others, are essential in our conception of municipal law. You have your own laws in this great community. Your laws would not possess the slightest value, they would not be worth the paper upon which they are recorded, if they did not carry with them the certainty that the malefactor who violated and defied those laws would be corrected by the strong hand of the State. Think next what it would mean to humanity if the great nations of the world could establish some kind of public law which, without corresponding precisely (that would be impossible) with our private law, would nevertheless give to those who come after us some guarantee that law, and not anarchy, will determine the relations of nation to nation, just as, in the gradually developed processes of our civilization, the rule of law has superseded the wildness of anarchy.

But the difficulty in dealing with International Law (again borrowing the purely technical language of the older writers on jurisprudence) has always been that there has been no *sanction* in our public law— and sanction, as you very well know, is the

9

term technically used to express the penalty which is imposed on the wrong-doer. A man breaks the law either on its civil or criminal side. If it is a civil matter, the plaintiff issues his writ and obtains his redress. If he breaks the criminal law, the methods are more summary. But the first thing to grasp about public law, about International Law, is this : That there is no sanction (with two tremendous reservations, which I will illustrate and attempt to explain in a moment), there is no sanction, there is no means of involving in the web of punishment the malefactor at the bar of Nations.

Consider what that means. It means this : If an individual nation chooses to say at this stage of the history of the world, " I refuse to be bound by your laws," civilization is impotent as against that nation unless (and these are the reservations to which I referred a moment ago), first, the other nations of the world are prepared to combine in war against this nation, and unless, in the second place, they are strong enough to combine success-fully in war against that nation. For it must be noted that if they fail, having com-bined against this moral anarchist, the wrong-doing is consecrated by successful war, as certainly as wrong-doing would be consecrated under the law of this State of New York if a gang of malefactors in the streets defied your police, and ultimately, on that defiance being challenged, defeated your police.

And we should further remember that it is not of itself paradoxical that a resort to armed violence should be necessary to vindicate law. Similar phenomena are, in ultimate analysis, recurrent in its domestic vindication. But in the field of domestic law observe this: The civilian authority must, if disobeyed, use force, or, in the alternative, must confess itself to be powerless before the assertion of naked anarchy. That is the real distinction, and in this crisis of the world's affairs its obvious relevancy is the sole justification of the somewhat commonplace observations to which I am asking your attention to-night. Bear this in mind, first, last, and all the time: The moment there is a violation of your municipal law, either you repel it or your city, and all the complicated structure of civilization which depends upon it, cease to exist. The moral anarchist must be dealt with, and must be dealt with at once. Either

9*

he makes an end of you, or you make an end of him. It may, therefore, occur to some of you to ask, since the points of distinction between private law and public law are so manifest, " How is it that through the history of the world so much effort has been made to lend the appearance of legal form, and to attribute, so far as may be, the appearance of legal sanction to the public law of the world ? "

It has not been because those who have spent their lives in attempting to create the edifice of public law were unaware of those weaknesses that they have nevertheless thought it worth while to labour constantly in order to make good the admitted defects of public law. They have known its weakness well. No legal writers have brought more humanity, more learning, or more shrewdness, to the study of the law than the publicists who have, by their collective contributions, made International Law at once a legal and a literary science. As many of you well know, an immense literature has grown up dealing with the science of International Law. It has been my habit for twenty years of my life, and my duty in the last three years as principal law adviser of the British Government, to keep myself generally acquainted with the chief authorities upon International Law. Indeed, it gives me satisfaction to say, addressing my brethren of the Bar of the State of New York, that in my humble judgment the greatest book that has been written upon International Law was that edition of your own Wheaton, which was enriched by the learning of Mr. Dana. And, gentlemen, you were not alone in your contributions to the literature of this subject. The best legal brains, certainly the best academic legal brains—and they were by no means the worst legal brains of the world—have created a vast intellectual product which contains and enshrines, in a worthy, and I still think a permanent monument, the industry that has been contributed to the literature of International Law.

I may, perhaps, give you an illustration of the growing authority of its doctrines among civilized countries : It has come home to me more closely than I could expect it to come home to American lawyers. It is well known to you that prize courts are supposed to administer not the laws of their own country, but International Law, and that their discharge of this trust is a test of their honesty and integrity. I, as Attorney-General, had recently to argue— such was my duty—before the Privy Council in Great Britain, that Orders in Council, proceeding from the Privy Council, were binding upon the Judicial Committee of the Privy Council. I argued that case. It had been argued before my day, in the days of the great Lord Stowell, I suppose the greatest intellect which in a judicial capacity has devoted itself in our country to the doctrines and problems of prize law. Lord Stowell refused throughout his career to decide that question adversely to the contentions of the Crown. Those contentions were the same contentions which I, as Attorney-General, put before our Privy Council two years ago, namely, that no prize court in Great Britain had the right to challenge or call in question the Orders in Council of His Majesty, delivered through his Privy Council.

Well, gentlemen, our appellate Prize Court, the Judicial Committee of our Privy Council —and it is not for me to say whether, in my judgment, they were right or wrong— decided after long argument against my contentions as Attorney-General. And they decided (whether they were right or whether they were wrong) to the credit of the integrity of the judges of Great Britain, for they said in effect : " We sit here as a Court of International Law, and in spite of what our enemies have done we still believe there are binding doctrines of International Law, and sitting here as we do sit as a Court, whose duty it is to construe those doctrines, we utterly refuse to be bound by Orders in Council issued by the Executive." (Applause.) " And if you force us by Act of Parliament, as you can, to recognize your Orders in Council, we will recognize them because we must, but it will become clear to the world that we have ceased to be a court which administers International Law, and that we have become the mere mouthpieces of executive and legislative authority in this country."

Allow me to observe that this was a decision which your judges, as far as I am acquainted with your reports, and I have studied them very closely—never gave in your great Civil War. It was a decision which the great Lord Stowell and their lordships of the Council, who sat in appeal from the decisions of Lord Stowell, never gave. I believe it is the first time in the history of war, and under the stress of a war which has made great demands upon judges —who, after all, are human—that this decision has been given to the world with the authority of the highest Prize Court in a civilized country : " We are a court ; we administer International Law, and we are not to be dictated to by any executive, even our own." (Applause.)

In the attempt to construct upon the foundation which was always known to be in one particular unsound, what it was hoped would, nevertheless, be a satisfactory and permanent edifice, the statesmen of your country and mine made immense efforts to arrive at conventions and treaties in which the conclusions of public law should be authoritatively stated. With that object we met at The Hague and other conferences, and the laws of war, by land and sea, were exhaustively examined by some of the ablest men in our countries, and on the Continent of Europe. And in pursuance of the same aims and objects, a complex network of treaties was formed.

It is worth while asking in the light of the cynicism prompted by our knowledge of the developments of this war : What justified the prodigious expenditure of moral and intellectual energy which was lavished upon these discussions and these conferences ? I think I can tell you almost in a sentence. The justification was the belief shared by almost all the civilized powers in the world that no power in modern times would be wicked enough to profess and even boast of a moral anarchy ; that no General would ever write, as Bernhardi wrote : " Treaties are only binding as long as they are beneficial to those who had signed them ; " that no monarch would ever say, as the Kaiser said to your Ambassador Gerard, in a cynical sentence, secondary and subordinate to the more important messages he was conveying : " Besides, there is no more International Law ; " and that no Power would be found vile enough to act as Germany did, when her legions swarmed in an orgy of blood and lust over neutralized and inoffensive Belgium.

And yet, Mr. Justice Hughes, we ought not here to-day, composing an audience in which sensible Anglo-Saxons meet, to hold ourselves wholly excused for our blindness. The country to which I belong is not generally supposed to consist completely of fools.

(Laughter.) Nor is the nation whose Bar in the State of New York I address usually described as one of symbolical simplicity. (Laughter.) We had our warnings in all these years, and our fathers and our grandfathers had their warnings. Let us not limit the indictment—the arraignment of simplicity—to one single generation : Silesia, Poland, Denmark, France and Austria cried aloud through the ages a bloody and plangent admonition to those who had ears to hear. Bismarck, the greatest and the most characteristic exponent of the Prussian and Junker class, was never tired of bespattering International Law with expressions of public contempt.

Had those who represented my country, and had those who represented your country, possessed eyes that could see and ears that could hear, during those critical periods in their history, this crisis might have been avoided. Had there been clearer vision in either country, we should have seen that there was growing up among one of the most powerful nations of the world, a deliberate and a proclaimed intention to substitute the maxim *sic volo, sic jubeo,* for the ordered and agreed body of Public Doctrine. We should have detected the barely concealed reversion, in progress before our eyes, to a perverse, but coldly philosophical, creed of anarchical violence.

This moral declension is generally admitted to have dominated the public thought, the history and the philosophy of Germany, certainly for a period of forty years, and probably (though with interruptions) for one of almost one hundred and twenty years. It deserves a cold and critical analysis. It serves no purpose in an assembly of lawyers merely to abuse the tendency. We have never, as a profession, been lacking in the arts of invective (Laughter); but to abuse this moral abnormity serves no useful purpose. You might as well pass a vote of censure upon appendicitis. (Laughter.) The real truth, if we look facts in the face, is that we are to-day (your country and mine, and the whole civilized world) face to face with phenomena which have been recurrent at long intervals in the history of the world. At intervals in that history the swaddling clothes of existing boundaries are burst, or torn, by the conquering elements of some mighty, challenging, martial race. Sometimes the soldier race which has swarmed over its frontiers has been civilized. Sometimes, barbarians have submerged an existing but less warlike civilization. The history of the world shows at least thirty occasions at which, at long intervals, victorious hordes have swept in conquest over contiguous portions of the world which they thought they could conquer, and of which (or so it seemed) policy suggested the conquest.

The success of such conquering empires has usually depended upon a number of conditions. It has depended, first, upon the possession of great military strength, the fruit of national character and national training. Secondly, upon the existence, in the polity of the aggressor, of a despotic form of government—for democracies will not, as a rule, permit the requisite preparations, or sanction on principle wars of aggression. And the third condition of such success has been the general absence, or the obsession, of moral standards in the conquering country, which, according to the circumstances, is the result either of natural savagery, or, where the conquering state has been civilized, is the result of cultural perversion or debauchery.

In a small number of cases, the condition has sprung from the legitimate desire of a higher type, emerging late in history, to assert its due place in the contemporary race.

I think that I have exhausted the circumstances under which these great conquering movements in the passage of generations—sometimes two or three centuries elapse between them—have stamped their consequences upon the features of the world.

They have arisen very rarely, as I have pointed out, but they have been generally very decisive in their consequences. It is, therefore, important to analyse the nature of the movement by which we are all confronted to-day.

If it were possible to say that the world-conquest movement initiated by the German Empire to-day fell under the fourth class which I have indicated to you—that is to say, a movement springing from the legitimate desire of a higher type, emerging late in history, to assert its place with resultant gain, upon a reasonable balance, to the human race—if it were possible to make that claim, we should be less severe critics of the tiger-spring which the German Empire has made at the throat of Humanity.

But we all know that there was nothing in the whole world denied to the German

Empire in the early part of 1914. There was no part of the world to which its citizens were not welcomed as colonists ; there was scarcely one where they were not the admitted conquerors in the peaceful arts, even where your great nation was a competitor. And I believe that when history pronounces its last condemnation of the German nation, it will conclude : It was insanity which seduced them into a moral perversion so abominable, and which involved them in a destruction so complete. It was the corruption of the soul which led them in 1914 to flout and mock the moral law of the civilized world. (Cheers.)

But that law has been most plainly challenged. It has been challenged neither by your country nor by mine. What is the challenge ? It can be simply and plainly stated. It is, in a word, the claim that might is right; that there is no public law; that a nation may break adrift from every recognized rule, and by brute force assert, in the first place, its superiority to law, and, in the second, by that unpunished assertion of force, win public recognition of that superiority.

I attempted in the first part of my address to call your attention, familiar though these subjects must be, to the essential quality of domestic law in every civilized country; and then I attempted by way of contrast, to exhibit to you the weakness of public or International Law, in that it did not possess the sanction necessary to involve the wrong-doer in punishment for that wrong. For the last two or three hundred years, most civilized countries decided on the whole that it paid better to observe International Law. It has been the glory of your country throughout its history, that it never broke an obligation of International Law, as that obligation was construed by the courts, your highest courts, or by the leading statesmen of your country.

It would have been as absolutely impossible for a great statesman in your country to go before his fellow countrymen, as it would have been for a great statesman in my country, and say: "We made that treaty, but the conditions have altered; it does not pay us to observe it. We propose to break it." I have had, as far as a stranger may, some reasonable knowledge of the history of your country, and it has been my business, at intervals to study the history of my own country, and I say that you could not discover a democratic audience of

Englishmen, or a democratic audience of Americans, before whom an English statesman or an American statesman could say, " True, we pledged our word ; but it does not pay us to keep it and we are not going to keep it." Such a Minister would have been broken in England ; such a Minister would have been broken in your country. (Applause.) And in this controversy so brutally developed, the consequence follows which is often found when bitter and fundamental antagonisms emerge, that compromise seems to be almost inconceivable. We conquer the anarchical element in public law, or the anarchical element in public law conquers us. Observe the issues which are developed here : Either law wins, either a result happens following upon the clash of arms, on which it is possible to say that, among nations as among individuals, the plighted word, the sanctity of contract, hold ; or the contrary follows. The consequences to civilization are so tremendous that I have no hesitation in saying that issues so vital to the whole history of the world have never been developed in any of the great wars of the world. (Cheers.)

The world has known dynastic wars, it

has known territorial wars, but it has never groaned under a war which has so completely challenged and put in issue the whole fundamental basis upon which civilization, humanity and Christianity depend ! (Loud cheers.)

If this be so, what is the test of success ? The test of who wins is found in the answer to the question : who is punished ? There is no other test. The court, some of you may say, in our legal phrase, has been constituted *ex posto facto*, but the League of Nations, as I understand it, and (I think) in the sense in which your President uses the term, is even now engaged in the work of retribution. Give me leave to add this : If we are determined—your country and ours, and our brilliant and inexhaustible ally, France (Great applause)—if your country and ours, and our Allies, are determined to go to every extremity, we must win. I do not dwell to-night upon the measure of our ultimate resources, if and when those resources are asserted in their final strength. I would rather, at this moment, dwell (though both are important) upon the moral than upon the material resources of the Allies. (Applause.) I say this, addressing the representatives of a great nation which has never tasted the bitterness of defeat in war—(Applause)— I, representing unworthily the British nation, say here, boldly and plainly before you, that we have played, as we shall continue to play, our part in this war ; and with your indulgence as friendly critics, I say, further, that it is a part which is unworthy neither of our past history nor of the alliance which you now extend to us ! (Prolonged applause).

I cannot say of my own nation, as I have said of yours with indisputable historical truth, that it has never tasted defeat. (Laughter.) But I can say this : It has only tasted it a very long way from home. (Applause and laughter.) And a long time ago. (Laughter.) And at a time when the tonnage difficulties were almost as great as they are to-day. (Laughter.) But I can say this of my country : In all its history, in all the bitter struggles in which it has been engaged, when once it has clasped in loyal faith the hand of an ally it has never faltered until the common quarrel has been carried to a successful goal ! (Cheers.) And as the humble mouthpiece here to-night of the British Empire I bring you this message : " Reinforced and comforted by your alliance ; clasping the hands of this country in our common peril, we say : Whatever happens, whatever the cost may be, of blood and treasure, whatever mortgages we draw upon the vitality of our race, and upon our future resources, this quarrel goes through to the death ! (Prolonged applause and cheers.) Here and now it finds a decision." (Loud cheers.)

Gentlemen, if we win and if we punish those who have broken the public laws of the world, International Law will have received a supreme public vindication. Perhaps no nation, however strong, will ever dare again to dream of aggressive war. Perhaps—I do not know—perhaps the great and splendid dream of an international tribunal, administering a law which would satisfy the analysis I have already examined, may be realized. Perhaps, I say, these things may happen ; I do not know. Our examination as lawyers of the noble proposals which have been made by your President, and which have been most warmly and sympathetically received in our country should be reserved, critical, but, as far as may be, helpful. If we do not coolly measure the difficulties which attend these proposals, attractive as they are, it is certain that those difficulties, swiftly and unexpectedly emerging will overwhelm the proposals, for—make no mistake—they are stupendous in their aggregate weight. Nothing but the importance of the result could persuade the world to try and solve a problem which seems so insoluble.

It is not my purpose here to-night to play the part of a pessimist in relation to hopes which may seem to many of us to afford the sole prospect of a happier world as the fruit of this war. My only object, as a lawyer addressing lawyers, is to call attention to the dangers of trusting rhetoric alone, to the immense difficulties which attend in practice the proposal to form an effective League of Nations. When I indicate these difficulties I do it, not in the spirit of a man who wishes to exaggerate their force, but of one who wishes, as far as he can, to suggest any method by which they can be overcome ; and I hope it will not be supposed that I am attempting to do anything but assist the proposals of the President when I ask you never to lose sight of the prodigious obstacles which lie in the way of the attainment of the ideal, so eloquently and so persuasively indicated by that great man.

In the first place, there is the difficulty of

limiting the armed force of each country, of allotting the appropriate contingent for defensive purposes to each country which will be represented at the Conference. I have read something of old European Conferences, and it may be that their laconic character will be more marked when they have American representatives among their number. (Laughter.) I do not know ; but it appears to me that the discussion as to what is to be considered an adequate military defensive force for each country is one which is likely to be protracted and most highly controversial. But I observe in this connection that a very distinguished statesman of yours has quite recently indicated a hope that national service will not be ruled out of the scope of the recommendations which the League of Nations may ultimately present. I have been all my life, under changed and earlier conditions, an ardent advocate of national service. I merely doubt whether that particular ideal is very much admired by those who are among the warmest supporters of the League of Nations.

I find it hard to reconcile the League of Nations with the survival of national service. If the League is effective there is no place for

universal national service. If it proves in-
effective, there will be growing need of it
both in your country and mine.

There is a further difficulty, that of dealing
with the special case of insular powers, and
the problem, involved in that case, of sea
power. It would obviously be no part of
my purpose to-night to exaggerate the difficulties which may arise in this connection.
But I should not, I think, be dealing can-
didly with you if I did not indicate, as matters
to be borne in mind by a very ingenious community, fertile in contriving remedies, that
great complexities are certain in this matter.
For instance, at the present moment the
American Navy is exhibiting all its old qualities of initiative and endurance, with results
which are not very easily distinguished from
the work which is being done by the Grand
Fleet to-day, and some of your ships are, as
you know, engaged on the same tasks in the
same waters. It is quite obvious, that a
complete change of view in relation to the
meaning of the phrase : " Freedom of the
Seas " would require both considerable discussion, and clearer definition than it has
hitherto received. To most of us it seems
that at this moment the American Navy is

fighting, with all its old valour, for the freedom of the seas. (Cheers.)

Furthermore, a great field of difficulty needs to be considered in another connection : The definition and allotment of air-power in the future. Gentlemen, the construction of airplanes admits of very ready concealment, and the phrase which has become as stale to me, as I suspect it has become stale to you, may still, for want of a better, be employed : the construction of airplanes is very easily concealed by camouflage. And yet airplanes, swooping in unexpected fleets, may very easily in the developments of ten years involve a whole community in complete destruction.

I confess I feel that there is a more fundamental difficulty—not that I am attempting to convey to you that I think these or any other of the difficulties are insurmountable :

The difficulty I have in my mind is one which will test the constructive wisdom both of our statesmen and of yours ; it is suggested by any proposal to stereotype the present tenure and ownership of the world's surface. I suppose that if a League of Nations be formed, it must start upon the basis that aggression is to be forbidden, punished, rendered impossible by the force of such arms as remain available in the hands of the League for collective employment. Here again, I am by no means to be regarded as standing in antagonism to these proposals, but only as recommending to you a careful consideration of all that may be involved in them. If, indeed, the League of Nations is to be invited to oppose a barrier to any further aggressive warfare, it is at least wise to recall some of the experiences of history. It is well to remember that empires wax and empires wane ; that a nation puissant and glorious, in one century may live to administer in another, with nerveless hands, an imperial heritage for which, in the long cycle of centuries, it is no longer fit. Such experiences have happened, not very remotely, in your contact with the Old World. Is such reconstruction to be undertaken by a Council of the Nations ? If it is, I sincerely trust that it will be unanimous in its decisions. (Laughter.) I do not know whether its members will vote equally, I do not know whether, when they have voted, there will be acquiescence in their decisions. Will great and proud nations lightly consent, in obedience to such a decision, to transfer territories, once the brightest jewels in their diadems, to a worthier legatee ? Would Spain so have agreed twenty years ago ? Would the League have compelled her ? Could you have obtained agreement from its members for that coercive purpose ? Would you have desisted from your purpose if that mandate had been denied ?

I do not know whether our present enemies are to be members of the League, or whether, if they are, they will strengthen either its influence or its credit. Will a Prussian, crouching for a second spring, be an agreeable bedfellow ? Is an unpurged Germany a possible member ? Obviously no—only a punished Germany ! So, by every route, we are driven back to the one static feature in a dynamic controversy : Public law disappears for ever from this world if we are proved powerless in this controversy to castigate the wrongdoer. (Cheers.)

Yet, I agree that it is worth while trying for the ideal.

It is worth while to make the attempt. It is better to harness your wagon to a star than to a machine-gun, though a knowledge of the one may be very useful as a means of

attaining to the other. I am not a pessimist in these matters. But I urge upon you,
as one cautious by temperament and training,
and slow to adopt rhetorical phrases, as a
substitute for the detailed working out of
problems, I urge that it is important, if
you cherish, as I know this nation dearly
cherishes these ideals, to prepare now. Get
the best minds of your country working now
to help this League of the Nations to bring
to tortured Humanity the first faint whispers
of an imperishable hope ? Believe me, it will
be far too late when the actual Peace Conference meets. (Cheers.)

Conceive the immense congestion of their
discussions ! Your President has claimed—
a claim which will neither be disputed nor
questioned in any of the Allied countries—
that the discussions of that Peace Conference
shall be public. I hope that I am not a
cynic, but my observations of discussions
has been that it does not invariably happen
that public discussions are the shortest.
(Laughter.) It may sometimes be so, but
I have known of other cases. (Laughter.)
If this Peace Conference, whenever it happily
meets, is to determine the whole territorial
reconstitution of Europe, upon lines so

admirably indicated, both by our own Prime Minister and by your President ; if it is to perform its prodigious work under the stimulus of publicity, so that each speaker developing a meritorious—and it may be an eloquent—argument, is aware that not only those who listen to him, but the Press of his own country will be preserving records of his sagacity and prescience, I have a feeling that the territorial discussions alone will occupy a considerable period. And if in addition the Peace Conference is to reconstitute the moral arrangements of the world, I cannot help thinking that the prospect will be more hopeful if some of the preliminary spade-work is done while the war still lasts.

Mr. Justice Hughes, I am deeply concerned to make my position clear to you ; and I have almost concluded my demand upon your patience. I am not here to disparage the most noble ideals, which, with restrained but penetrating eloquence, your President has uttered for the encouragement of his Allies, and the refreshment everywhere of well-intentioned men. But I am here as a lawyer addressing lawyers. We are careful and cautious men, and if we do not apply the touchstone of critical analysis, what can be

expected from the rest of the population ?
(Laughter and Applause.)

I myself am concerned to make this sure—
that instead of merely talking about a League
of Nations which is to render war impossible
hereafter, we shall, as far as assiduous attention and forethought can do it, consider
before the occasion actually arises, whether
such a thing is or is not in the range of human
endeavour. Do not let us give up hope or
surrender enthusiasm, too easily. It would
be a black prospect if out of this war we
plucked no sure and certain hope that we
might avoid the horrors, and the obscenity,
and the cruelty, of war for our sons and grandsons. And, indeed, if this ideal be ever won,
it will be because we have anticipated difficulties in time to crush them. But, if it be
attained, a precious salvage will be redeemed
even from the Pit of Despair. Without
posing as a prophet in reference to hopes,
which at this stage of the world's anguish
must be pronounced very shadowy, I make
bold to say that I clearly descry, even in this
black gathering of clouds, one bright lining.
For centuries there have been occasions of
coldness between your country and mine.
This war will not have been waged in vain if

these two proud and free nations, which have so often misunderstood one another in the past, learn, as they march side by side along a bloody road, of which the milestones are graves, the secret of an immortal—an indestructible — harmony. (Prolonged applause.)

GOVERNOR CHARLES E. WHITMAN : Mr. President, there is very little that we, the Members of this Association, can do to express to the honoured guest of the evening, the speaker, our appreciation of the great speech to which we have listened ; and the welcome which is his from all of our people in our City, and in our State, and in our land, a cordial welcome which is his, and which awaits every worthy representative from the great country from which he comes.

On behalf of the Association, I desire to move the election to Honorary Membership of the New York Bar Association, of Sir Frederick Smith, Baronet of the United Kingdom, Attorney-General of England. And we realize that we are honouring ourselves in honouring him. (Applause.)

PRESIDENT HUGHES : Under our parliamentary procedure, that motion requires no second.   All in favour of electing Sir Frederick Smith, Privy Councillor, Attorney-General of England, to Honorary Membership in the Bar Association of the State of New York, please manifest it by rising.   (All rise.)

You are duly elected, Sir Frederick.

SIR FREDERICK SMITH : I addressed you, when I began my remarks, in a conventional sense as my Brethren at the Bar of the State of New York ; I now address you, with deep satisfaction, in a more literal sense, as my Brethren at the Bar.   I do not know how things may develop in London.   Human affairs are notoriously mutable.   Even Attorney-Generals lose their office.   If I should lose mine, it may be that I shall come to this State to avail myself of my membership of your Bar.   (Applause.) But I tell you very seriously that I have received your kindness with great emotion. (Cheers.)

JUDGE HUGHES : They measure ships by their displacement, and I cannot harbour the thought of the displacement which will be occasioned in the New York Bar if Sir

Frederick should come among us ; but none the less, we should welcome him then as much as we welcome him here to-night. Nothing refreshes lawyers so much as a straight talk from a hard-headed lawyer, with clear eyes, with vision and aspiration, but treading firmly on the ground, walking erect, man-fashion, not blinking at any difficulty. With our hands in the hands of Britons, and Frenchmen and Italians, and in the hands of men like Sir Frederick, whom we have welcomed to-night, we will conquer a peace, and we will stay together until that peace becomes permanent. (Applause.)

CHAPTER X

Sunday, January 13th.—I was to have
been accompanied to the mass meeting at
Chicago by Secretary Lane, but his boy, of
whom I have already spoken, was under
warning to sail for France. He is in the
Flying Corps, and his father was naturally
anxious to be with him until he sailed. By
a series of strange chances, his departure was
postponed week after week, and he ultimately
left New York by the same steamer which
carried us to England. I was fortunate in
making his close acquaintance.

When we awoke in the morning, we found
that Mr. Arthur E. Bestor, president of the
American Publicity Department, was on
board with his secretary. He proved upon
acquaintance to be a very agreeable and
resourceful travelling companion, himself
possessing very considerable powers of speech.

Col. M., H. S., F. E. S., Arthur E. Bestor,   J. Davis
(Solicitor-General U.S.)

[To face p. 160.

The train was late in reaching Washington, but, on our arrival there, we were joined by the Solicitor-General of the United States, John W. Davis, whom I had met at Washington and of whom I have already spoken. Mr. Davis was to take the place of Mr. Secretary Lane at the great meeting at Chicago. He had been described to me by more than one judge of the Supreme Court as one of the few men in the United States of America, and indeed in any country, who could argue really difficult and subtle questions of law with lucidity, and even with brilliancy. I was to find at Chicago that he united to this precious gift the power of swaying by moving eloquence an audience of many thousands. Such a man in any country must go far, and I predict for him a very remarkable future. He is still only in his forty-fourth year.

There also joined the train here Lieutenant McDonald and his orderly, Alley. We did not at first conjecture the purpose of this gentleman's presence, but we were not left long in doubt. He had been before the war one of the best known " movey " photographers in the States. He joined the Army as a volunteer before the war broke out, and was attached to General Pershing's force in

Mexico, taking photographs from aeroplanes. In this pursuit he spent many months and was about to resume the same dangerous occupation in France. The present tour was a little interlude which he was to use to gain some photographs of the tour for the American Publicity Department, which in the end very kindly presented me with a film for reproduction—" if anyone cared to use it " —in England. McDonald was certainly a very remarkable operator. He was always first out of the train, always standing grinding away at his machine at unexpected moments, always apparently in complete control of the railway stations and the streets and every-one in them. And afterwards, when he accompanied us to Canada, we were amused to notice that the same authoritative instruc-tions commanded the same docility from Canadian citizens which he had always been able to secure from his countrymen. He was a merry, assiduous, and most obliging companion. Good luck go with him !*

Monday, January 14*th.*—We reached Chicago at 1.30, nearly five hours late, and again in detestable weather. Another terrible

---

* Nearly all the photographs produced in this volume were his work.

blizzard had visited the city since we left,
and, still more serious—a third was predicted
as certain to arrive early that evening, which
was the night of our great meeting.   And the
place of meeting was by no means in the
centre of the city, and was hopelessly inconvenient if the street traffic was interrupted.

It is hardly necessary to say that Samuel
Insull met us at the station and took us to
lunch.   At 4 p.m. the Chicago Bar Association gave a reception to the Solicitor-
General and myself.   It was attended by
about four hundred and fifty members of the
Bar.   Davis and myself both addressed them,
after which, at 6.30, we went to dine again
with Insull at the Chicago Club.   Here once
again we had the pleasure of meeting T. P.
O'Connor, who afterwards went with us to the
meeting.   The speeches at dinner, to which
we both contributed, were mercifully short.

The scene of our exertions in the evening
was the Medinah Temple, and we were
relieved to find that, in spite of the weather
and the warnings of the Press, five thousand
people were present.   Many had been turned
away.   It was an inspiring sight ; and no
man could wish for more kindness and more
enthusiasm.   The Solicitor-General insisted,

against my wish, that I should speak first. In the middle of my speech, I predicted, as a consequence of this war, eternal friendship and mutual esteem between our countries. The Solicitor-General, with a warm-hearted impulse, stood up and grasped my hand, and for five minutes the audience stood and cheered itself hoarse. This was a public meeting, without tickets of admission, and in Chicago! Insull told me that he was not surprised, as the change in opinion in Chicago in a few months had simply been incredible. The Solicitor-General followed me. I think it is always hard to speak second at a great meeting, where the first speaker has inevitably taken the earliest enthusiasm of the hearers. But Davis, who spoke for thirty minutes, made a really fine speech—well reasoned, forceful and marked by serious and restrained eloquence.

The inexorable conditions of our travel once again asserted themselves. Our train was due to leave for Louisville at 10.30. We went to the station and were advised that it would be at least two hours late. Nothing seemed less attractive than Chicago's station in that weather at that hour. So we went, under advice, to a very interesting restaurant

—" Morrisson's Supper Café "—for supper. All the tables were arranged in semi-circular tiers, rising to a height of perhaps twenty feet. In the centre was a stage, on which a very fair musical entertainment was in progress. Occasionally the professionals deserted the stage, which had no barrier separating it from the guests, and the latter were allowed with their friends to dance on the abandoned platform. It was rather a pretty scene. After supper to the station, but again the train, like the Ausonian Tiber, grew more and more remote. And in the melancholy sequel we had to wait two hours until the private car which the Government had " loaned " to us was discovered. At the time it seemed a particularly bad joke that it had actually been lost in Chicago's station for three hours. I was finally seen fast asleep on a bench, between two people who were speaking German and eating oranges. Four children surrounded us. The Lieutenant retrieved me. And I was too tired to mind. So away at 3.30.

Wednesday, January 15th.—We arrived at Louisville at 6 p.m. Seven hours late. We had barely time for a bath before dinner at the Seelbach Hotel. About three hundred persons were present. Bestor and myself made speeches. After dinner we were joined by Doctor George E. Vincent, one of the celebrated " spell-binders " in the United States, who had been assigned to me as a travelling companion by Washington, when Secretary Lane was compelled to relinquish the tour.   He is a very interesting man, a scholar, an accomplished speaker, a wit, and a very entertaining conversationalist.   Formerly President of Missouri University, he gave up that distinguished position in order to become President of the Rockefeller Foundation.

After dinner we went on to the Macaulay Theatre, a large building, holding, I suppose, about three thousand people, which, as usual, was crowded, even to the gangways. We were told that it was a thoroughly representative meeting of the State of Kentucky, as invitations had been sent to and accepted by prominent persons in every part of the State.   It was a very enthusiastic meeting. Doctor Vincent spoke for about forty minutes. He speaks incomparably more rapidly than any speaker I have ever heard, but always finishes his sentences, which are carefully formulated and, as one would expect, with a

Posing, by order of the Lieutenant, after a breakdown in Nebraska.

[To face p. 166.

fine literary flavour. He has a good deal of humour, and a countless fund of stories of a whimsical kind. It would be hard to imagine a more effective speech for such an occasion. The meeting was over at about half-past nine. We paid a brief visit to the Louisville Club, and left to catch our train at 10.40 p.m., and so to bed.

Wednesday, January 16th.—We arrived in St. Louis at 9.30 a.m., too late for our connection. The Government had authorized us, in case any difficulty of this kind threatened an important engagement, to take a special train. We accordingly did so. Our faithful old friend, Judge Taylor, who had been waiting just to shake hands with us since 7.30 at this draughty station—think of it !—just had time for fifteen minutes' talk before the train left.

At 7.30 a.m. the engine suddenly ran into a big load of wood which a farmer had casually left on the line, as it proved (a little unfortunately) too heavy for his team, just at this particular point. The shock was very great, and our cow-catcher was considerably bent. We had to stop for repairs, and during the delay the engine-driver told me that we had narrowly escaped a bad accident. For if the point of the cow-catcher had pierced the earth, the engine might easily have turned turtle.

We arrived at Columbia, Missouri State, at about four o'clock. We were met, amongst others, by President Hill, a most charming man, fifty years old, but looking much younger, able and cultivated. Our first engagement was to address three thousand students of the University in the theatre, which is part of the University, and is, I believe, the largest public building in the State. The meeting was very crowded, and consisted of students of both sexes. Half the young men were in khaki. The President told me that he would not have been able to keep any of them, had it not been most gravely urged upon the students that it was the duty of every young man to wait his turn under the draft, accepting on this point the judgment of the authorities, and not following his individual impulse. He told me that, even so, there was much unrest and dissatisfaction among the young men whose turn had not yet arrived. "A spirit of fever," he added, "is abroad among them all. They keep hearing from their friends and relatives in the camps, and they will not be satisfied that their place is here."

This was quite a different audience to any I had hitherto addressed, and I confess that I found myself face to face with so much radiant youth, in a season so melancholy, with a good deal of emotion.

I told them of our own Universities; of Oxford, Cambridge and the rest; of Quadrangles where the grass no longer grew, bruised by the feet of young soldiers, of colleges in my own University, whose conditions recalled that other bitter quarrel when Charles I. made his Court at Christ Church, and his Queen hers at Merton; and I told them, too, of the long Roll of Honour, which showed that the hearts of our University boys were as stout as their fathers' had been. And then I told them, with deep sincerity, of the pity I felt that their youth had not been suffered to enjoy without tragic interruption the most careless and the happiest period of their lives, to

" Chase the blossom of the flying terms."

It was their hard fate to live in one of those cruel periods of the world's history, when the State in self-defence was driven to approach its young citizens with the message : " You are the children of a great Country, arise, the time has come to defend it."

They listened in great earnestness and solemnity. When I had finished, they sang their student song with a vehemence of fire which I confess brought the tears very near my eyes. *Eheu morituri !*

After the meeting, I had an interesting talk with the President, on the subject of the co-education of the sexes in America and in Universities, where there are residential hostels for both boys and girls. He told me that the intercourse was easy, wholesome, and almost unrestrained. The boys had their clubs, known as brotherhoods, the girls theirs, known as sisterhoods. The clubs would entertain one another at tea, or on other occasions. No rule prevented members of opposite sexes from visiting theatres together. He was hardly aware of a single case of scandal having occurred in any American University as a result of this system. The feeling, he explained, and the atmosphere were felt to be against it. The relationship was almost a family one.

The old University had a very fine façade, supported by noble Corinthian pillars. It was burnt down many years ago. But the pillars survive, and lend a most picturesque appearance to, the present University, reminiscent of some old Greek temple jutting over the blue Aegean.

We went back to the hotel for dinner, and prepared for the evening meeting, which was also to take place in the theatre. But none of the students was allowed to be present at this meeting, as it had been specially arranged for farmers. Tickets had been sent to nearly every important farmer in the State of Missouri, and I was told that no more important meeting of the agricultural interests had ever taken place in Columbia.

I spoke to them on two subjects only. First of all (this by request) of the broad, general issues underlying the war; of the causes which had been sufficient to involve in its horrible conflagration two nations so wedded to peace as Great Britain and the United States; and of the immense consequences to civilization of the permanent good understanding between the two countries which seemed a certain consequence of their brotherhood in arms.

I had been told in New York that there was considerable ignorance among the farmers of the Middle West. I must say I could see no signs of it. No audience could have been quicker in taking points, although, of course, one does not expect the same volatile demonstrativeness from rural audiences.

And then I told them—and this at length—of the conditions of agriculture in England; of the efforts we had made with our depleted man power to increase the area under corn cultivation; of agricultural labourers who had flocked to the colours; and of the thousands of gently nurtured young women who were ploughing in our cold, autumn fields, and mastering the coarsest tasks of agricultural life. And I told them, too, of the women of France; of the corn supply of France; reduced simply because the men were needed for the trenches; how I had seen over and over again old women, patiently and bravely ploughing the modest family holding, while the shells screamed overhead. And then I spoke of the conditions in Great Britain, Italy, France, Belgium, Rumania and Serbia. And I spoke of the submarine campaign and its effect upon the food supplies of the Allies. And I concluded, "You have come at a gloomy moment, as the Allies of a melancholy and suffering brotherhood. You and you alone

can save them. They will not appeal in
vain to the generous farmers of America.
I shall return to my countrymen and tell
them that if your sacrifices and your exertions
can achieve it, succour will be forthcoming
to them according to the measure of their
necessity."

One result of this appeal was a little
embarrassing. I had to shake hands with
most of the farmers who were present at the
meeting, before they left the hall, in order
that each one might tell me what he had
already done, and what he intended to do.
It took a very long time, but, be sure, I did
not grudge it.

And an hour after I reached the hotel, I
received the following resolution :

ASSOCIATION OF THE FARMERS OF
MISSOURI.

The Executive Committee of the
Farmers of Missouri who have given
their sons to the draft to fight for the
Allies, assures the Attorney-General of
England that they have already made
an immense increase in the area under
corn cultivation. They assure him

further that they will strain every effort to increase still further their contribution to the food necessities of the Allies. They thank him sincerely for his speech."

Mr. Vrooman, the Under-Secretary for Agriculture, made a very able speech at this meeting. He did not deal particularly with agriculture, but made a very optimistic speech upon the whole war situation. In particular, he much encouraged us all by predicting a period in which the American aeroplanes, blackening the skies like locusts, would sweep down upon the German lines until they were completely blotted out. His prediction that after the war one of the tasks awaiting the United States would be to feed the populations of the Central Empires was, I thought, received with considerably less enthusiasm.*

The deep spirit of earnestness which distinguished the meeting may be illustrated by the fact that it opened with a long and eloquent invocation by a local clergyman, and ended with a prayer, which, in its turn, was of adequate length, but very impressive.

* And at the moment it would appear that our enemies are giving some attention to this problem themselves.

And so again, at eleven o'clock to the train, which had begun to seem our home.

Thursday, January 17th.—The arrangements made for us in Kansas City and Topeka were broken to us when we reached the train last night, and nearly produced the first strike of the tour. Mr. Bestor, our impresario, had secretly made the following programme : 7.30 a.m., Public Breakfast at the station, with an address to our hosts the Chamber of Commerce ; nine o'clock, Speech at the Garden Theatre ; one o'clock, Speech at Topeka ; eight o'clock, Mass Meeting at Topeka. The intervals he had considerately left to ourselves.

This was indeed an exacting programme, coming on top of our travels and exertions of the last few weeks ; but we were advertised in all these places, and remembered, as people, who are not scholars, can always in compensation remember " tags " :

> " Quidquid prohibere est nefas,
>   Levius fit patientia."

We were met at the station by many kindly citizens at Kansas City, Missouri. It is a great and growing city with 400,000 inhabitants.   This part of the town is wet; the other part, on the other bank of the river, in Kansas State, consisting of about 100,000 people, is dry.   The resultant complications are considerable.

A large number of business men and lawyers—again I say, " Oh, wonderful Nation ! "—were assembled with warm kindliness at 7.30 at the breakfast, which was extremely good, being served in a refreshment room belonging to a firm whose name I have forgotten, which supplies the railway systems the whole way to San Francisco, and which, I am told, is the best in the United States.

The mass meeting at the Garden Theatre at 9 a.m., was, I think, the most trying experience I had the whole tour, but the good nature and kindness of the audience carried us through.   Vincent, Bestor and I, all spoke.   But it was trying us very high.

H. S. had been greatly pressed to address the undergraduates of the University of Kansas, so we dropped him at Lawrence for the purpose, arranging that he should rejoin us at Topeka.   He had a very fine meeting, his experiences much resembling mine before the students at Columbia.

We arrived at Topeka, where it was raw and extremely cold, about 1 p.m. Here we were met by Governor Capper, the proprietor of the leading local journal, and evidently a man of great influence and reputation in the State. I was told that he was one of those thoroughly patriotic American citizens who hoped against hope, almost to the end, that some means would be devised whereby the States might be kept out of the war. But the Germans convinced him, where many other rhetoricians had failed, and he has thrown himself into the cause of the Allies with all the resources of a most powerful personality. He took us to the Rotary Club luncheon, where, I suppose, some three hundred members were assembled. We were late, and lunch was over. But we were in time for the speeches, and in a very few moments, as the phrase goes, for the third time that day I was " on my feet." Then, in mercy, I was taken to another room to get some lunch. I returned an hour and a quarter afterwards and made a remarkable discovery. Only four of the whole original party were left. Of these, one was eloquently addressing the other three. But an old member of

12

the House of Commons, who has sat through many dinner hours, cannot easily be deceived. I saw at once that there was a silent, but honourable, compact that, as each remaining orator concluded his remarks, he should remain to form an audience for his patient colleagues. And once again I thought of the passage from the *Dialogue*, which I have already quoted, and of Juvenal's hackneyed

" Semper ego auditor tantum ? "

In the afternoon, we walked round the town with Governor Capper, who took us to the very elaborate office of his n wspaper, and then to the Capitol, which is a fine modern building. In the evening we dined with the Governor and his lady, and had a very pleasant evening. Later, we went to an enormous mass meeting, consisting, I should suppose, of more than four thousand people. The two sisters of General Pershing were present on the platform, and I was presented to them. A very good military band played, and a choir of girls sang the " Star Spangled Banner " most beautifully. It is indeed a melody fit to express the spirit

Lincoln, Nebraska.   The Chief Justice.

[To face p. 178.

of a great people.   The Governor made a fine
fighting speech which carried the audience
to a great pitch of enthusiasm. I spoke
next, and Dr. Vincent after me. He firmly
refused to speak anywhere but last, though
I often urged him to begin the meeting.
He would always good-naturedly reply that
this was my show.

Mrs. Capper and a friend of hers, who had
dined with us, and whose boy was just sailing
for France, then drove us to the station in
a light-powered electric car, which made
very heavy weather of the snow.

We parted from them with great regret,
feeling as if they were old friends, and left
at about midnight.

Friday, January 18*th.*—The journey to
Lincoln, Nebraska State, from Topeka, is
only about two hundred and forty miles, but
we did not arrive there until 2.30 p.m., which
cannot be accounted a very brilliant performance on the part of the railway. We
were met by the Chief Justice, the district
Attorney-General and Professor Fogg, the
Professor of Rhetoric at the University of
Nebraska.

We drove to the Lincoln Hotel, and I
then went, as I always do if time allows,

12*

to pay my respects to the Principal of the local University. The Nebraska University is one of considerable reputation, containing in normal times nearly three thousand students of both sexes, with residential houses. We met Dean Elliott and Chancellor Avery. Their statistics of the number of students serving were almost exactly similar to those given when describing the effect of the war on the University of Missouri. But the American Universities have two advantages over British Universities. In the first place, as already pointed out, the draft works gradually, and, in the second place, the numbers of the female students are hardly affected by the war.

We dined at the Lincoln Hotel, where a large party of lawyers and men of business were assembled. I spoke for a quarter of an hour, and immediately after dinner we went to the meeting, which was so crowded that many hundreds were turned away. I suppose it would hold, packed as it was to-night, three thousand people. I was met in the ante-room by twenty or thirty former students, now in khaki, who led the way to the platform, bearing aloft on great poles the American colours, a demonstration which it may be imagined caused considerable excitement.

One becomes weary of praising meetings, and afraid of using exaggerated terms, but we certainly addressed no finer meeting in our whole tour.

Late at night—and a very cold and unattractive night—Professor Fogg, the accomplished Professor of Rhetoric, most kindly came to say good-bye to us in our car. We kept him till long after midnight, when the train left, engaged in an interesting and at times animated discussion as to the merits of the great figures in American literature. Personally, I dislike these comparative valuations of authors, but did not decline the discussion with so kind and cultivated a host. I put forward Walt Whitman, Edgar Allan Poe and Hawthorne as the three greatest figures in American letters. As to Hawthorne he agreed. The Professor was not apparently a great admirer of Whitman's writings, or at any rate of " The Leaves of Grass." I know what he means, but I have thought it for twenty years (and still think it) a work of great genius. He objected to Edgar Allan Poe that he did not represent an American type of letters. This seemed to me a bad objection. For instance, as I pointed out, the Germans claim Shakespeare, but he was born at Stratford-on-Avon. He nominated Washington Irving and Long-fellow (accepting Hawthorne), a selection which decided me that no basis of com-promise existed. So we parted from one another, friendly but unconvinced contro-versialists.

I ought to add that the Chief Justice of the State had taken the greatest care of us at intervals throughout the day and evening. I had a long and interesting talk with him about the Courts of his State.

Saturday, January 19*th.*—Once again we are on our way to Chicago, due to arrive at 4.30 p.m. The train is late and we do not draw up at that station, which we are learn-ing to know so well, until 7.30. It is hardly necessary to say that Samuel Insull has given up all his engagements for the evening in order to give us dinner. He met us at the station with the English Consul-General, who had been the first to receive us on our earliest visit, and was, like Insull, in at the death. We dined again at the Chicago Club, and had a quiet and pleasant evening, rendered more agreeable by the reflection that our labours were nearly concluded, and that the next eight or nine speeches* which I had to make would be to Canadian audiences, and, though the main subject would be the same, one would be able to approach it from a slightly fresh angle. I had, indeed, exhausted in the thirty speeches which I had made almost every conceivable method which I could imagine of presenting the issues of the war to American audiences, since as the character of the audiences did not as a rule vary very much, and the speeches were reported at considerable length, it was very difficult to attain to a continual freshness of treatment.

Many speakers feel no delicacy at all about repeating a speech of an hour over and over again, with the same jokes and the same thrills of emotion. It is a little hard to suppose that this method is consistent with that freshness of contact which is so great a part of the charm of good speaking. But I remember, when a boy of eighteen, hearing a King's Counsel, who is now a Judge, make a speech on Home Rule, which I had no doubt was the bravest, the wittiest, and the most eloquent, I had ever heard. It carried me off my feet. Over and over again the

* This proved too sanguine an estimate.

audience broke in (and I did, too) with almost hysterical laughter. And I still remember the shock with which, being at Birmingham a week later, I read the same speech, in the same language, with the same jokes, and the same tears. But I still have no doubt that it was a very fine speech.

We had now left for ever the private car which the American Government had lent us, where we had spent so many tedious hours, but to which, nevertheless, we had often been glad in our weariness to return. We were now to exchange it for another fine Canadian car which we owed to the courtesy of the Ministry at Ottawa. We found this car waiting for us at the Grand Trunk Station, and just before midnight we began our journey for Canada.

I was last in Canada in 1912, travelling as far as Winnipeg with Lord Beaverbrook and my dear and valiant friend Edward Horner, who was killed the other day.

I break off once more from the diary to offer some general observations upon the subject of Canada and the contribution of Canada to the war.

And I may be forgiven here for saying—now that every Englishman has found

Canada—that fourteen years ago I formed the resolution that I would never visit the United States of America without also visiting our friends in Canada, and though I often travelled in the States I never broke this habit, and I never will; it is a good working rule for every Englishman.

CHAPTER XI

THE POSITION IN CANADA

IT is well known that the statesmen of Germany did not believe that Great Britain would be able to obtain effective help from the Dominion in the event of a European war. In the first place, they did not think that the Dominion could give help if they would, and in the second they did not believe that they would if they could. General Bernhardi said quite plainly in his book that the Colonies would be wholly unable to play any effective part in the next European war. Those of his countrymen who have happened to meet the Canadians at Ypres and the Vimy Ridge, or the Australians at Pozières, will be in a position to put a right value upon the prescience of the gallant author. There was, perhaps, a little more excuse for the second delusion. Our own statesmen, and historians of the highest consequence, had shown for generations a complete inability to realize the strength of the roots which the home country had cast into the soil of her self-governing dominions. The greatest of English political writers, Burke, in his passionate efforts to avert the breach with our American settlements, had indeed bequeathed to his countrymen a conception of the relationship between mother country and dependency as tender as it was imaginative. But his effort, in its particular application, was a tragic failure, and to most of those who came after him he was unable even to transmit the spirit of his message. The Victorian era had the vaguest understanding of the outer dominions. An occasional relic of the Botany Bay spirit was to be found when a magistrate remanded a more than usually incorrigible young criminal " to see if a passage to the colonies could be found for him."

I do not recall—though I write without the certainty afforded by a library—one single passage in the speeches even of that robust patriot, Palmerston, which shows any real understanding of the British Empire. Gladstone's views are well known. And although the brilliant imagination of Disraeli made him more than any other man the political legatee of Burke, from whose ideas, indeed, he borrowed even his title, yet even he, in a sentence of despair, once seemed to contemplate the inevitable dissolution of the fabric of the British Empire. The whole influence—very powerful for a generation— of the Manchester school was thrown in the parochial scale. One imagines that Cobden and even Bright would have welcomed the news that every self-governing colony of the Empire had issued a Declaration of Independence, fashioned upon the model of that with which Washington confounded the politicians who surrounded King George III. And a very gifted historian, Professor Goldwin Smith, who, ironically enough, chose the city of Toronto in which to spend the evening of his brilliant life, was never tired of lavishing the resources of a sarcastic pen upon the relations subsisting between the Motherland and the Dominion. " What is the use," he cried, " of Colonies whom you dare not tax, and who will not fight for you ? "

With such encouragement from so many persons of consequence in England, it is not surprising that the Germans should have supposed that the devotion of the outer dominions would not support the strain of a great war. And yet, a study of recent history might have suggested doubts. In the very darkest periods of the South African war, Canada had sprung to arms with a devotion, and a passion, which should have struck the imagination of the whole world. And the troops were Canadian who, at the very crisis of the war, stormed with invincible valour the trenches at Paardeburg, behind which sullen Cronje had at last been brought to bay.

When the present war began, the statesmen of Canada realized with swift intuition that the whole future of the Empire was at stake. And in appealing to the people of Canada, they were playing upon a willing and a noble instrument. Lieutenant-General Sir Samuel Hughes, K.C.B., the Minister of Militia, was one of a band of men (of whom I may also mention Colonel Denison) who had always advocated the closest union for all practicable purposes with the Mother Country. And General Hughes had spent his life in acquiring, according to his opportunities, the art and practice of war. No one played a greater part at the beginning of the South African war in raising the Canadian contingent, and no one discharged his military duties with greater

promise than the Colonel Hughes who commanded a battalion in that force. The
General is no longer Minister of Militia. But
what has been, has been. He has had his
hour. Nothing can ever take away from him
the credit for the energy, the resource, and
the driving power, which called together
so swiftly the first immortal Canadian division and improvised, like an Eastern wizard,
the camp of Valcartier. A large proportion
of those who sprang at once to arms, were,
as was natural, of British origin. But the
whole nation, with a well-known exception,
followed ; and at the present time, from the
comparatively scanty population of Canada,
500,000 men have worn the uniform of the
King. Sir Wilfred Laurier threw the whole
weight of the Liberal party in the same
scale. Differences have since emerged between this great Liberal statesman and Sir
Robert Borden — differences which have
found their solution in a general election.
The Premier had formed the conclusion that
the Province of Quebec was not making its
proper contribution to the armies of the
Dominion, and he was of opinion that such
a contribution would not be forthcoming
under a voluntary system. Sir Wilfred

Laurier took a different view. Many of his most trusted Liberal colleagues parted from him upon this issue, and are to-day members of Sir Robert's government. The constituencies have pronounced upon the issue. It is generally believed that Quebec will loyally acquiesce in this decision, and it would be obviously improper for an English politician to offer any opinion upon a domestic Canadian question. But, while recognizing the prescience, the courage, and the spirit of personal self-sacrifice shown by Sir Robert Borden, we may be allowed to assure that distinguished veteran, Sir Wilfred Laurier, that no Englishman ever doubted either the depth or the purity of his patriotism.

Three and a half years have passed since Canada took the fateful decision. In that period, one of the greatest empires in the world has grown war-weary, and is to-day staggering in a welter of anarchy. The steam-roller of affliction has passed over Belgium, Serbia, and Rumania. Dynasties have fallen, and the red atmosphere of revolution grows apace. But the spirit of courage in Canada is still to-day as bright and far-flung as the mantle of her winter snows. She has suffered in proportion to her numbers as deeply as Great Britain. She has lavished the best blood of her youth as freely as her accumulated treasure. She has developed for war purposes a resource of manufacturing ability of which no one could have supposed her capable. She has supplied incredible quantities of shrapnel to the Allied forces. She is to-day manufacturing small arms and uniforms for the infant armies of the United States. And her courage and resolution grow day by day. One household in Vancouver has sent fourteen sons to the armies of the King, a contribution which I believe to be unique in all the armies of all the belligerents.

All the cities of Canada have done well. But the loyalty of Toronto is traditional, and as I happen to have before me some material which shows what Toronto has done, I select it as typical of the whole.

Since October, 1914, when it became obvious that the dependents of Canadian soldiers were in many cases in need of financial help, the citizens of Toronto have busied themselves in making a suitable provision. They have carried on four campaigns, in the last of which I was fortunate enough to bear a small part, in order to raise a sufficient fund. The aggregate result of these four great efforts was a sum of $9,793,000. In addition to this, the citizens of Toronto have contributed to the British and Allied Red Cross and Relief funds, $3,077,000. The City Council has made grants in aid of one or other of the above funds to the amount of $6,000,000. To this must be added the local expenditure upon the Toronto Y.M.C.A. in France, amounting to $500,000. The amazing total of all these contributions amounts to no less than $19,370,000. In order to appreciate the full significance of these figures, it must be pointed out that the population of Toronto consists of 473,000 persons, so that the city has contributed nearly $40, or £8 per head, of the population, including every man, woman and child in Toronto. Nor is this all. Toronto has raised sixty battalions at a cost of $20,000 each, making in all $1,200,000. The city has already disbursed to dependents of the 2,836 killed $2,798,000, making a total of $3,998,000. If the two great totals, as given above, be added, it will be found that the total contribution to the war of this astonishing city amounts to $23,368,000, or nearly $50, or £10, per head of the population.

And the effort is as surprising if it is tested
by the figures of voluntary enlistments. The
number of volunteers from Toronto was
60,000, from the county of York, 20,000 ; or
80,000 in all. And the Toronto contribution
works out at one in nine of the population
of the city.

A further illustration is afforded by the
record of the University of Toronto. From
first to last, there have served with the forces,
of the graduates and undergraduates of the
University, 3,000 officers and 1,500 men.
The Professor of Architecture is a major of
infantry, who has been wounded after long
service in the trenches. There have been
killed in action, or have died on service, 330 ;
550 have been wounded, missing, or have
been made prisoners. One student has
gained the Victoria Cross, and 330 honours
of different kinds have been won by members
of the University.

I cannot resist in this connection quoting
from a letter written to Mr. Briton Rivière
by the late Professor Goldwin Smith in 1889 :

> " Canada never has given, and never
> will give, a penny to Imperial arma-
> ments ; and she herself, relying on

Imperial protection, is totally without the means of defence. In case of war she would be a dead weight in England's arms. In fact, a maritime war would to a moral certainty terminate the political connection, and in a very unhappy way."

Mr. Haultain, the editor of the Professor's "Correspondence," says of him in the Preface : " He saw far—very far." He would have found it easier to support this claim if he had suppressed all the Professor's ill-natured and extremely inaccurate predictions as to Canada.

It must never be forgotten that the splendid military distinction which has been gained by the armies of Canada has fallen to an army of which nearly all the officers, including those of general rank, are civilians. I do not know how many brigadiers there are in the British Army, who were not regular soldiers when the war broke out ; and I am told that in the whole British Army no rank superior to that of brigadier is held by any amateur soldier or civilian. I have never heard it suggested that the armies of Canada are not competently led. With the exception

13*

of the highest command of all, the generals of Canada are lawyers, editors, men of business, or real estate dealers. And these have confronted on equal terms the instructed products of the most scientific military school in the world. And they have not suffered by comparison with their British colleagues.

In the face of efforts such as I have attempted to indicate, and which could be paralleled in other parts of the Dominion, language of acknowledgment is useless. All Englishmen are proud, and rightly proud, of the supreme exertions made at the crisis of their fate by these little Islands. And, musing upon the incomparable efforts made by that daughter, who is yet " mistress in her own house," we may exclaim :

" Matre pulchra filia pulchrior."

Our new car, amongst other comforts, contains a bath. I cannot imagine why every private car does not possess a shower-bath. Apparently all Ministers of importance in Canada are allowed a private travelling car, which must be a considerable comfort. It costs one in the States thirty ordinary fares to take a private car. Not more than four or five can be comfortably

The Governor-General on his rink.

[*To face p.* 196.

stowed away, so that the excess cost is very considerable.

If one cannot take a private car, the only hope is a drawing-room car. Failing that, one reposes in the Indiscriminate Saloon. And hence sleep and privacy withdraw together.

We arrived at Port Huron, the frontier, at 11 a.m. Here Bestor left us on his way to visit his relatives. He practically arranged the tour we had just completed, and did it extraordinarily well. He has been with us for exactly a week, living with us day and night in the curious intimacy of train life. He has a great sense of humour, is extremely good-natured, and has, in every way, been an agreeable companion. He would be a very suitable person to organize and bring over to this country a number of American speakers.

At 5.30 we arrived at Toronto, where we were to stay at Government House, as the guests of Sir J. and Lady Hendrie.

The other guests were the Governor-General, Harold Henderson, the Duke's Military Secretary, Captain Ridley, one of the A.D.C.'s, and Sir William Mulock, K.C.M.G., a retired judge, now occupied in the administration of the Military Service Acts.

Government House is quite modern and extraordinarily comfortable—particularly in relation to those minor details which are so well understood in the New World, and so badly in the Old. It has a splendid ball-room and many interesting portraits of former Governors. The Governor and Lady Hendrie are most kind and friendly, as is Miss Hendrie, who gave capable instruction to some members of the party in the more intricate of our modern dances. We had an amusing dinner, after which some of us played bridge. Sir William Mulock gave the Colonel in the conservatory an exhaustive explanation of political and many other matters in Canada.

Monday, January 21st.—H. and I walked three and a half miles into the town for exercise. We had no " rubbers " and it was a most dangerous performance walking in the ice and snow without them. Lord Richard Neville, the Duke's Comptroller, broke his leg by slipping in the snow a few months ago ; he spent six months in hospital and he will certainly always be lame.

We called at the Toronto University to pay our respects to President Franklin, who received us with the greatest kindness. He gave us the information about the University which I set out in the last chapter. He showed us the University buildings, which were new to H. but not to me. A melancholy but glorious tablet in the entrance hall recorded the long list of the fallen. We then went to Trinity College to see the Dean, H. T. S. Duckworth. Years ago, he had been the head boy at Birkenhead School (under the Rev. A. Sloman, the Editor of *Terence*, once Master of the Queen's scholars at Westminster, and an ex-President of the Oxford Union*), at a time when I was a moderate-sized boy in the fifth form, and H. a very small one. I remember that Duckworth gained a Postmastership at Merton College (where I was one day to be a Don), and that afterwards he was placed in the first class, both in Mods and Greats. He was the show figure at school in my young days. We had a long talk about old times. I reminded him that, shortly after he left, the upper sixth, reduced in numbers, consisted of five boys only, of whom four— his brother, L. Duckworth, M. W. Patterson, C. T. Wood and myself—all subsequently obtained Fellowships at Oxford or Cambridge.

* I shall be forgiven for recalling here how much I owed, as a boy, to his teaching and inspiration.

We agreed this must rather be a record, even for the greatest of schools. The fifth boy was A. F. Robson, who went to Trinity College, Cambridge, as a Sizar. This is a wholly unjustifiable digression. Let those quarrel with it who have forgotten their own school days, and the joy of reviving these fugitive memories far from home.

We lunched with the Canadian Club, which had taken St. James' Hall for the purpose, in order that the general public might come in afterwards. The galleries were quite full and the body of the hall packed. The Chairman told me that it was the largest gathering in the history of the Club. Among those present were the Premier of the Province, Sir William Hearst, the Lieutenant-Governor, Sir William Mulock, Chief Justice Falconbridge, the Attorney-General, and General Sir Sam Hughes. He has always been a faithful friend of mine, though I often—very often—disagree with him. I had not seen him for two years, and had a long talk with him about Canadian politics and Canadian military affairs. He is, I am told, a tenacious enemy. I can only speak of his simplicity and fidelity in friendship. No one has ever denied that he possesses a rugged and most striking personality. And all his life he has devoted himself to arms and the Empire. He may have been wrong upon many sma'l points, but surely he has been right upon the great point where philosophers and statesmen have been wrong.

I also met John Carrick, whom I had last seen as a colonel on the Canadian Staff in France. At our last meeting he, I, Lord Beaverbrook and—by a coincidence—the Colonel of this tour, argued about the length of the war (how wrong we all were!), at the Hôtel de Commerce at St. Omer, early in 1915.

I spoke for about forty minutes, leaving the luncheon table with the Chairman for that purpose and mounting the platform. I spoke almost entirely about what Canada had done in the war. The subject, inexhaustible to an Englishman, was a welcome change to myself after so many speeches addressed to audiences in the United States upon a topic which, so far as my resources went, I had completely exhausted.

After lunch Carrick took me to Sir Donald Mann, Vice-President of the Canadian Northern Railway Company. I had hoped to see Sir William McKenzie, but he was out. Sir Donald, most hospitable, gave me some cigars. We had a good talk with him about the war, and the future development of Canada, a subject upon which he is, as one would expect, extraordinarily well-informed. All his domestic servants are Chinese.

In the afternoon, the Bar of Toronto had arranged a reception at Osgood Hall. This was the first occasion on which, as Attorney, I met Canadian lawyers. There were many present whom I had led in the Privy Council, and some who, in the old days, had led me. The Treasurer of the Association presided. He is a fine old man, eighty years of age. There was a very large attendance. The President introduced me to the members collectively. In the middle of his speech some prominent person would catch his eye, and with the attractive simplicity of an old and courteous gentleman, he broke off to call him up to be presented. I made a speech all about law. Very dull. But I made it, I think, towards the close, arresting by telling them of the numbers of English lawyers who had fought and died in the war, and of the long list of honours which they had won. But here they had their own record. Afterwards, I was introduced individually to many of the judges and leading members of the Bar. Judge McLaren, of the Appeal Court, also a veteran, told me that when he first appeared before the Privy Council, he was junior to Benjamin, and when he last appeared, leader to Haldane. A remarkable record. I meant to ask him, but forgot, how the Board was constituted on his first appearance.

We dined at Government House, before the large meeting at Massey Hall, where an extraordinarily fine audience of about five thousand people was collected. It was very moving to see so many of our own folk. Mulock was in the chair. The Duke, as he always does, made a very sensible speech. He is treated everywhere with deep respect, partly, of course, due to his office, but largely to his high conception of public duty. Those whom I addressed were as quick in taking points as an audience at the Town Hall, Birmingham, or the Sun Hall, Liverpool, and full of enthusiasm. It was the first mass-meeting I ever addressed in Canada, and having regard to the record of the city, I am glad that it should have been at Toronto.

After the meeting we left for our car, where, among others, Sam Hughes joined us, also on his way to Ottawa. The Governor-

General travelled by the same train, in his own car. We left about 11.30. Hughes came round to our car and we talked to all hours.

Tuesday, January 22nd.—We arrived at Ottawa at 11.45, three hours late, and left in the two motors for Government House, where we were to stay with the Duke. The last time I had stayed with him was at Chatsworth in 1910, when I had arranged to speak for Kerry. By an odd coincidence I was three hours late on that occasion too, my car breaking down in the snow over the hills of Derbyshire. So that I came to them twice through the snows.

Government House is an old-fashioned, rambling building, which has been added to by successive Governor-Generals. It is, on the whole, very comfortable, and has some beautiful reception rooms. The Prime Minister, Sir Robert Borden, whom I had known well for many years, had asked us to lunch with him at the club. He had invited about thirty guests, including all of the Ministers who were in Ottawa at the time.

The Coalition was indeed almost completely represented. Among the Conservatives were J. D. Reid, Minister of Railways ; Arthur

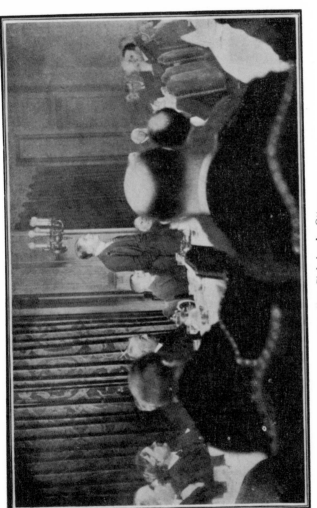

Canadian Club lunch, Ottawa.

× The Governor-General.

[*To face p.* 204.]

Meighen, Minister of the Interior ; C. C.
Ballantyne, Minister of Marine ; S. C. Mew-
burn, Minister of Militia ; J. A. Calder,
Minister of Immigration ; A. Sifton, Minister
of Customs ; Martin Bunell, Secretary of
State, and T. W. Crothers, Minister of
Labour.

Among the new Liberal Members of the
Government were N. W. Rowell, President
of the Privy Council ; Sir Thomas White,
Minister of Finance, and T. A. Grenar,
Minister of Agriculture. And there were
present many judges, including the Rt. Hon.
Sir Charles Fitzpatrick, Chief Justice of the
Supreme Court. All the Ministers, including
the Premier, spoke in the highest terms of
the ability of Arthur Meighen, Minister of
the Interior. He was formerly Solicitor-
General, and is, I suppose, a " political
lawyer." But unless I am mistaken, he
will play a great part in the history of
the Dominion of Canada.

I sat next to Sir Robert with Sir Wilfrid
Laurier on my other side, and I certainly had
a most interesting lunch. It was my fault
if I did not understand Canadian affairs
when it was over. The Premier and his pre-
decessor talked among themselves with much

cordiality and seemed on the best of terms. Sir Wilfrid, who is, in the tale of years, an old man, showed no signs of fatigue after his recent election campaign. On the contrary, he was alert, lively and most agreeable. He is, and will be as long as he lives, one of the great personalities among the Statesmen of the Empire.

I had last met Sir Robert Borden in 1916, staying with Bonar Law at his house by the sea. Winston, I remember, was of the party, and the present Prime Minister motored over on Sunday to lunch. This was on the day when we first had private news that Bulgaria was committed to the war. We talked over old times, and then all three of us discussed the war together. Sir Robert has always seemed to me to be not only a very sincere and direct, but a very resolute and imperturbable man. I suspect that his opponents have, throughout his career, made the mistake of underrating him.

Later, the Prime Minister introduced me in a very kind speech, and I did the best I could before this distinguished audience. Fortunately only a short speech was required.

After lunch, we went for a long walk to watch the winter sports. Tobogganers, skiers,

A skating group at Government House, Ottawa.

[To face p. 206.

and skaters. The scene was animated, and it all looked very amusing. We did not compete. I would like to have tried the ice-toboggan, but it was terrifyingly steep, and one had to pull the car back oneself up the steep mountain side.

In the evening, there was a large dinner-party at Government House, consisting of about forty people. The company consisted of a number of Ministers and judges, with their ladies, including Sir Robert and Lady Borden, and many of those whom we had met at lunch. I sat between the Duchess and Lady Borden.

The proceedings in the large drawing-room after dinner were formal, the Duke speaking to every lady at the party in turn, and the A.D.C.'s tactfully effecting changes among other groups, if at any time there seemed a tendency to stagnate. The proceedings, how-ever, left one with rather a bewildering im-pression of playing General Post.

The household at Government House is very friendly, and I should think works together with a most admirable harmony and loyalty. Lord Richard Neville is Comp-troller of the Household, and is kindness it-self to the Duke's guests. He thinks of

everything one may want, just before one
wants it.   Harold Henderson is one of the
military secretaries, an old colleague of mine
in the House of Commons, and almost a
neighbour in the country.   For many years,
too, we have been brother officers in the same
brigade of Yeomanry.   He has a convenient
little house at the end of the garden.   It was
nice to see Lady Violet and him again.   We
met at their house for bridge.

The A.D.C.'s are very attractive young
men.   One of them, Captain Ridley, a relative of my old friend, Mr. Justice Ridley,
was a planter in East Africa when the
war broke out.   He and his three partners
at once enlisted, and he fought in the
Tanga affair.   Two of his partners have
been killed.   He returned to England and
joined the Grenadier Guards.   Since then,
both he and his remaining partner have been
badly wounded.   Another A.D.C. was Captain Kenyon-Slaney, also of the Grenadier
Guards, and a son of that Colonel Kenyon-
Slaney who was so well known and liked in
the House of Commons twenty years ago.
Lady Helen Kenyon-Slaney is the daughter
of my old friend and political colleague,
the Duke of Abercorn, with whom I had

A false alarm after a halt on the track.

[To face p. 208.

stayed in Ireland. Kenyon-Slaney himself
had been badly wounded in the war. I
thought that both he and Ridley did work
which required both tact and judgment
extraordinarily well. Captain Bulkeley-
Johnston, of the Rifle Brigade, is another very
popular A.D.C. He is a nephew of Brigadier-
General Bulkeley-Johnston, of the Scots
Greys, who lost his life in France recently,
and was a most gallant soldier. Captain
Bulkeley-Johnston has himself been seriously
wounded, and is universally recognized as a
very promising officer. And indeed, I heard
on all hands how popular the whole household
was in Canada. The position, when they
went there, was by no means easy to fill, for
I suppose in all the history of Canada, no
occupants of Government House were quite
so much beloved as the Duke and Duchess
of Connaught. The Duchess was, indeed,
worshipped by everyone, and it would be
impossible to overstate the service rendered
to the Empire during their momentous period
of office by the immediate predecessors of the
Duke and Duchess of Devonshire.

And the Princess Patricia's Regiment have
for ever, as long as military history is written,
made glorious with their swords the name

14

of the gracious lady under whose favour they fought.

Wednesday, January 23rd.—We skated all the morning on the private rink at Government House. The day was bright and sunny and the air like a wonderful tonic. Nearly the whole party took to the ice, and it was very amusing. The Lieutenant was very busy with his cinematograph.

We went to lunch at the Country Club, motoring to the electric railway station, and thence several miles by a car which had been reserved for us.

The Club is one of the nicest we have yet seen. Originally a country house, it stands on the banks of the river, and it is proposed, when the war is over, to connect it by a bridge with an Island of Enchantment, owned by the Club, and like Ithaca, much wooded, where bathing and boating can be enjoyed under ideal conditions. The party consisted of about fifty of the members, including several Cabinet Ministers and Sam Hughes. The Committee, with the hospitality which distinguishes this most kindly people, had caused to be painted, and gave me, a water-colour drawing of the club house, to be a permanent reminder of a happy day.

At the Country Club, Ottawa. General Sir Sam Hughes and other friends.

[To face p. 210.

There were no reporters and I made an informal speech of about half an hour—for the first time in the whole tour permitting myself what the late Mr. Stevenson commended as " a little judicious levity."

In the evening there was another great dinner at Government House, consisting, as before, of about forty guests, of whom Sir Wilfrid Laurier was one. It was very pleasant, but resembled in its general features that which I have already described.

As a social observer, I amused myself by noticing how greatly the drought of these repasts reduces the period in which the men of the party find entertainment in masculine talk.

At eleven o'clock the hospitable Club where we had lunched had arranged a dance in our honour. It seemed, when the moment arrived, to be many, many miles away. I confess that I tried to run out, but was told (and this was true) that I had promised to go, and that the party was arranged on this understanding. So once again the motor cars carried us to the electric railway, on a windy journey in the snow, and we found, in compensation, a very gay and pleasant company assembled. Society in Ottawa talks good-humouredly of some of its youngest and most

14*

unruly members as the " Naughty Nine." I
suppose they may distantly correspond with
those young people in London (alas ! a
diminished company since the war) to whom
the name of " Souls " has, by an obscure
affiliation, descended. It means, I fancy,
only that a very innocent degree of extra
emancipation is claimed by its members.
We were told that many of the number
were present. I saw (without counting) many
delightful young ladies, but nothing to justify
the adjective.

We stayed on, Harold Henderson and
the A.D.C.'s and the rest of us, some dancing,
some talking, some playing bridge, until
about 4 a.m. It was, perhaps, at this
stage allowable, even for middle-aged men,
desipere in loco, for the tour, with all its
grinding exactions, was very near its close,
and the speeches rapidly coming to an end.

Thursday, January 24th.—In the morning
we skated again. Little Anne, the youngest
daughter, very sweet and self-possessed.

We lunched at the new hotel, the " Château
Laurier," with the members of the Canadian
Club. Judge Duff, one of the ablest members
of the Bench, who is to-day sitting in final
appeal over the decisions of the tribunals

A horse sleigh at Government House.

[To face p. 212.

in the Province of Quebec, was in the chair. Sir Robert Borden and many other Ministers were present. I ought to have said that Sir Cecil* and Lady Spring-Rice were staying at Government House. Sir Cecil, who is shortly returning, was present at the lunch. He is returning—but without his family— to London. He had himself—so I was told —addressed the same Club a few days before, and had made a deep impression by an earnest, sincere and unaffected speech. I can easily understand that he would get on very well with the Canadians. The room to-day was very crowded, the guests numbering, I suppose, between five and six hundred. And the gallery of the dining hall was crowded with ladies. I spoke, according to orders, for forty minutes.

We were due at the railway station for Montreal at 3.30. So we took leave with great regret of this kindly household, which, like poor Rupert Brooke's sleeping place, " is for ever England," and at 6.30 had reached our destination. It was bitterly cold when we left the station at Montreal. We drove in an open sleigh, with the temperature

* This was, of course, written before I heard of Sir Cecil's sudden death. I have not altered a word.

already below zero, to the Ritz-Carlton Hotel. I had always previously stayed at the " Windsor." The " Ritz-Carlton " is comparatively new, and is very luxurious and comfortable. Harold Henderson came with us, and Lord Richard Neville—which I thought extraordinarily kind—came over from Ottawa for the speeches next day. Sam Hughes saw the last of us at Ottawa, and had already sent a number of letters about us to his friends at Montreal.

Sir Charles Gordon had asked us to dine with him at the Mount Royal Club, which is one of the best clubs I know in the New World, with the indefinable atmosphere about it of a good London club. The dinner consisted of about thirty, and the company was very distinguished, consisting amongst others of Lord Shaughnessy, Sir Vincent Meredith, Sir Mortimer Davis, Sir William Peterson, the scholarly head of the McGill University, Sir Frederick Taylor, Chairman of the Bank of Montreal, F. E. Meredith, K.C., cousin of our valued friend, the British Consul at Detroit, and many others.

There were no reporters, but there were, of course, speeches. After I had spoken, Lord Shaughnessy made a blunt, forcible speech, expressing very well his personality, in which he laid stress on the importance, after the war, of evolving some constitutional arrangement under which, for the future, Canadians would be consulted in matters of imperial policy. Both Borden and Laurier have insisted upon this very reasonable claim. Shaughnessy put the case plainly but moderately, and his views evidently met with a large measure of support. I have no doubt (and I hope) that the Government of Canada will insist on this view after the war.

The President of the McGill University also spoke in a very interesting way. The whole evening was enjoyable. When it ended, we went to play bridge at Sir Mortimer Davis's house, and then to bed about three o'clock.

Friday, January 25th.—We lunched with the Canadian Club at the Windsor Hotel; about seven hundred people were present, and a number of ladies were in the gallery. Very many people, who could not get seats, came in after lunch. The room was unpleasantly over-crowded, but the spirit and good feeling shown extraordinary. I enjoyed this meeting as much as any which

I addressed in the whole tour. But so many people were turned away that I was, on the whole, sorry that we had not arranged a mass meeting on the scale of that which I had addressed at Toronto.

After lunch H. and I rushed off to play tennis with Sir Frederick Taylor and Gordon. The court was a covered building, with *en-tout-cas* surface, extraordinarily good. We had four sets ; then, hurriedly bathing and changing, I went to address the Women's Canadian Club at the " Ritz-Carlton " at 4 p.m. Mrs. Drummond presided over a very large meeting of nearly six hundred ladies. I tried to tell them of the work done by the women of Britain. But the women of Canada, I suspect, have little to learn even from so noble an example. It was sad to see how many widows were among the audience. But their spirit was unquenched.

And no sooner was this over than my friend, Sir William Peterson, was waiting to take me in a car to give an address to the students of the McGill University. Here again we found a crowded audience of both sexes. Many of the boys were in khaki. The contribution of the University to the war has been as glorious as that of the

University of Toronto. And of the boys
all are gone or going.

Here, too, the students sent me away to
the strains of their " Varsity Song."

In the evening we dined again with Sir
Mortimer and Lady Davis, and played
bridge till very late.

Saturday, January 26th.—I went shopping
with Lady Davis to buy light literature for
the voyage. Later we went with Brigadier-
General Sir Charles Gunning to see the
remount depot at La Chine. It was certainly a very remarkable sight. There were
about three thousand horses running absolutely wild in the enclosures. Shaggy and
unclipped, they seemed fit enough to jump
out of their skins. They galloped round
and round in mobs through the bush, sometimes three or four of them together jumping
the great drinking troughs. One could not
imagine pictures of more perfect health and
strength. And yet they were always exposed in the open, day and night, with a
temperature often twenty degrees below
zero. Certainly one can always learn something fresh about horses.

The British Remount Commission, under
General Gunning, has, I understand, been

subject to criticism, much of which is certainly uninformed. The French Society for the Prevention of Cruelty to Animals has attacked them for keeping the animals in the open in all weathers. I hold the view (which many other people have of themselves) that I am a good judge of horses and of their condition. I never saw fitter animals in my life. And the figures speak for themselves. The following table makes the matter plain :

HORSES

Total purchased................439,206
Shipped 381,709
Loss on land 7.53%
Loss on sea .... .53%

MULES

Purchased 268,685
Shipped 257,081
Loss on land................... 1.91%
Loss on sea................... .32%

So that the average loss per annum on all animals was 6.34 per cent. on land, and .46 per cent. on the sea.

The average daily strength of the horses in General Gunning's charge was 29,037. The average mileage from the purchasing point to the port of embarkation was 1,666

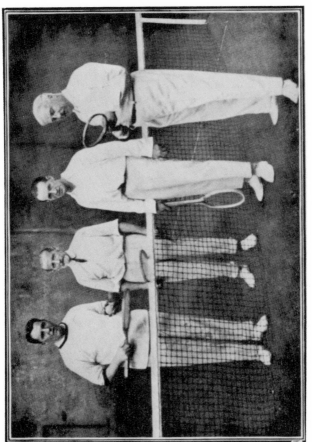

Lawn tennis at Montreal.

F. E. S.   Sir Frederick Taylor.   H. S.   Sir Charles Tate.

[*To face p.* 218.

miles. The average travelling time was eighty-seven hours. And as there were fourteen purchasing points and eight embarkation ports, the complexity and, it may be added, the success of the general work are patent.

We went to lunch with Sir Frederick Taylor. After lunch, again to the covered tennis court, where we had excellent games, Sir Charles Tate making the fourth.

Then to the skating rink, and afterwards to dinner quietly at the Montreal Club.

And at 8.30 we took a train to New York. The formal speaking was over. We had been advised that there was good prospect of a ship home. Accordingly, we returned for shipping orders, proposing in the interval to see again some of our New York friends.

Sunday, January 27th.—We have finished finally with the trains. From first to last we have travelled over seven thousand miles by railway, a distance certainly equivalent, under existing train conditions, to ten thousand miles. To this, of course, must be added the distance travelled by sea, which cannot, having regard to the devious and unusual route we followed, be put at less than seven thousand miles.

Once again we made our headquarters under the hospitable roof of Goelet, at 591, Fifth Avenue. We lunched with him at the Links Club, which is, I think, on the whole, the most attractive club—and I have knowledge of many in different parts of the world—that I have ever seen. It is quite small, and the membership limited. Two old-fashioned houses have been thrown into one, and the greatest ingenuity and taste have been shown in adapting the result to the purposes of a most comfortable and beautiful club. It is bright, cheerful, home-like and exquisitely clean. We spent a great deal of time there during these last few days.

They gave us at lunch what is known as "applejack." This is cider which has been allowed to mature for about six months, air being admitted by leaving the cork out of the bunghole of the cask. In the case of applejack, the alcohol is distilled by the regular "still" process. But a few farmers (as I have said) have another method. This is to separate the alcohol by means of a cream separator. The result is a most potent drink, seventy-five to eighty-five per cent. alcohol, about fifteen per cent. more powerful than absinthe. *Expellas furca !*

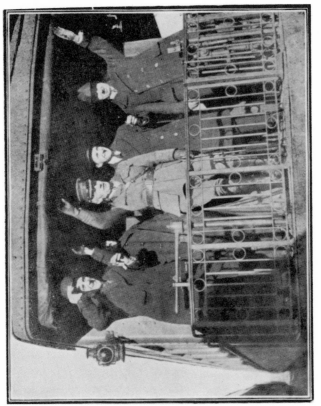

A farewell !

[To face p. 220.

In the evening we dined at the same Club with the same host, and later went to the Sixty Club Hall, at the "Ritz-Carlton." This Club consists very largely of members of the theatrical profession. Those who wish to entertain engage a table for supper and invite guests. Altogether there were to-night, I should imagine, as many as two hundred different parties. Many people, well known in New York, were present, and an extraordinary number of beautiful women. The war seemed very remote. But in such matters the psychology of the human race is very puzzling. Nearly all those present were either themselves, or had relatives who were engaged in the war. In the French Revolution, the victims of the guillotine amused themselves with unconquerable gaiety almost until the moment when they mounted its steps. In Paris, the craving for relaxation is by no means extinguished, though for more than three and a half years German trenches have been only fifty miles from the Tuileries. I suspect that the very horror and tension of the war induces a feverish reaction which breeds in humanity a restless groping after the appearance of gaiety. "If death indeed be so close," such perhaps is the psychological reasoning, " let us drink while we can every drop of the cup of life."

Monday, January 28th.—H. and I motored twenty-five miles with Mrs. Burdon and Miss Hollins, to Harry P. Whitney's house at Roslyn, to play tennis. The court is extraordinary. It is, of course, covered by a great glass roof, and forms part of a large building, which contains a studio in which one could dine fifty people, and, connected with it, plunge and other baths. The ladies played very well, and we had interesting games. Three sets in all : the first Mrs. Burdon and I won, 7 to 5 ; the second lost, 5 to 7 ; the third we lost, 12 to 14.

In the evening we went to the opera to hear Caruso. The immense Opera House was absolutely packed, the effect being extraordinarily brilliant. I saw many old friends in the boxes, but I do not understand music, and did not stay long.

Tuesday, January 29th.—Ben Ali Haggin had asked me to sit for my portrait, and accordingly I have given him several hours.

We dined to-night with Major Thwaites, of the Fourth Irish Dragoon Guards. Others of the party were Lieut.-Col. Sir William

Wiseman and Malone, who was formerly collector of the Port of New York. It was a very pleasant party. Malone is a very interesting, amusing, and hospitable man. He took us afterwards to the Lambs Club, a kind of Savage Club, which is full of actors, the grill being cooked by a prominent actor who appeared in chef's costume. Much simplicity and good humour.

Wednesday, January 30th.—I lunched with Mrs. Cornelius Vanderbilt, in the beautiful palace which, in its decorations, suggests Versailles rather than New York. Colonel Roosevelt was one of a small party, which included Major Mitchell, the ex-Mayor of New York, of whom I have already spoken.

The Colonel was in great form, and as they say in Scotland, " in full spate." But very vigorous and vital. We agreed on some points, though by no means on all, and had a friendly argument. He is sending me a copy of his speeches, which I shall value. I have read some of them; he certainly possesses, in a remarkable degree, the power of vigorous expression in nervous English.

As we had differed, though in the friendliest way, in some points, I thanked him, as we parted, for the noble and constant words of encouragement which, in the black days of the war, he had never ceased to utter to Great Britain and France. These things, I told him, never could be forgotten, and never would be. They were of the soul. He was certainly pleased, and, I think, affected by this.

We dined that night, at 8.30, with Charles D. McDonald, the banker, to whom I had been specially commended by my friend Urban Broughton, and who is the kindest and most warm-hearted of friends. The dinner was at the Links Club, of which he is President. There were about twenty guests, and I made the last speech of the tour.

They delighted me greatly by electing me a life member of the Club, an honour which I value very much, and of which I shall always avail myself whenever I visit New York. I have now two New York Clubs —one in the clouds, and the other " down town."

And so good-night and good-bye to everyone !

" Cras ingens iterabimus aequor."

CHAPTER XII

HALIFAX AND HOME

HERE the diaries cease. And there is little to be told now which the rules of censorship will permit. But the British Government is repeatedly causing it to be known that ships sailing from the States to England call at Halifax for various purposes. There can, therefore, be no indiscretion in saying that the vessel, by which we were to leave, took this somewhat exceptional route. I was not sorry to have the chance of visiting Halifax so soon after its terrible disaster. I had never been there before, as it is a little aloof from one's ordinary travels in Canada.

We arrived there in due course. Our ship was full of American officers and soldiers. Here again I conceive that I cannot come into conflict with any rule of the censorship, as it is well known to the Germans that American troops are being dispatched to France. We lay off Halifax for two days. None of the passengers was allowed to land, except the O.C. troops, the second in command, and my party. It was thought reasonable that we should all be permitted to pay our respects to the Governor.

Accordingly we went ashore, in very bitter cold, observing everywhere from the deck of the steam launch the devastating traces of this horrible calamity.

The cause of the explosion was a collision in the Narrows on Thursday, December 6th, between a French munitions carrier, the *Montblanc*, and a Belgian relief steamship. The *Montblanc* was carrying three thousand tons of high explosives, including more than fifty tons of Trinitrotoluol.

Just above the Narrows is situated the Richmond section of Halifax, the home of the working classes, who live in frame dwellings built closely together in narrow streets. The explosion took place after breakfast time. The entire district collapsed in ruins. Probably five thousand houses were completely wrecked. From fifteen hundred to two thousand lives were lost, though it is not even now possible to compute the losses accurately. All that can be done is to accept the number of those missing as an accurate guide. The corpses were still being exhumed, nearly two months afterwards, at the time of our visit. Five million pounds' worth of damage, so it is estimated, was caused.

In the Protestant Orphanage, the matron, three servants, and forty-six children were killed. This was almost the most ghastly tragedy of the whole explosion.

As showing the nature of the calamity, it may be added that at Ruro, sixty-two miles distant, the windows of the Learmont Hotel were broken and the clock was shaken from the wall of one of the offices.

Two American vessels, one a cruiser and the other a hospital ship, were fifty miles from Halifax. Both felt the shock with such force as to believe simultaneously that they had struck mines.

The explosion raised an immense tidal wave in the harbour, so high that it swept forty feet over the line of the Inter-colonial Railway, carrying off loaded cars like corks. I myself saw one which had been swept right across the Narrows, as if a giant had thrown it, from the Richmond, or south, to the north side. And again on the Richmond side there is a pier upon which the same titanic convulsion had flung a tug-boat, plucking it bodily from the water and leaving it high and dry on the jetty. As we passed by the charred and blackened ruins of the place where so much humanity had been blasted and destroyed in one second, I was irresistibly reminded of the ruins of Messina, which I had seen soon after the earthquake.

A special Court was set up by the Government to investigate the causes of the disaster. It was presided over by Mr. Justice Drysdale and the findings of the Court were made public on the morning we sailed. The court found that the master and the pilot of the *Montblanc* were to blame for the collision and its consequences. The Attorney-General of the State thereupon directed that a proceeding should be instituted against them for manslaughter, and these prosecutions are now pending.

On landing we went to Governor McCallum Grant's house, and were fortunate enouh to find him in. Government House is an attractive, old-fashioned building, about a hundred and forty years old, and contains in the hall interesting tablets recording the names of all the governors, French and

English, for about one hundred and sixty years.

We had a long talk with the Governor, who received us with great kindness and reminded me that Halifax or its neighbourhood was the birthplace both of Mr. Bonar Law and of Lord Beaverbrook. The latter's father, he added, was a Scotch Presbyterian minister, a striking personality, who lived much of his life in Canada.

He told us much that was interesting and terrible about the explosion. It had been necessary for the authorities to deal at once with the needs of twenty-five thousand homeless persons, in the middle of a bitter winter. There were, moreover, many terribly maimed persons who must inevitably die unless the slender medical and nursing resources of the city were swiftly and enormously reinforced. And immediately, without the loss of an hour, the State of Massachusetts performed one of the most splendid acts of philanthropy and charity which has ever alleviated the bitterness of a great misfortune. Mr. John F. Moors, director of the American relief work, was sent over by the Governor of Massachusetts without a moment's delay, at the head of a staff of medical men and nurses which comprised almost every famous surgeon and competent nurse in the State. All freely and gladly abandoned their own tasks and came to Halifax in its hour of agony. They brought with them stores, medical comforts, surgical implements, inexhaustible credits in money, and, best of all, the sympathy and the tears of a warm-hearted neighbour. And the Governor impressed upon me that the delicacy with which these services were offered was at least as impressive as their material value. " We are here," said Mr. Moors, " not to take charge of the relief or of the medical arrangements which you may think proper to make. That is the responsibility of the citizens of Halifax. We are here merely to act under your directions, to do anything which is in our power to help those who have suffered. Make known to us your wishes and we will attempt to carry them out. If there is anything which we have failed to bring with us, point it out; we will immediately obtain it." And it may be mentioned as a crowning illustration of the generosity of the American nation, that the State of Massachusetts has undertaken to provide and fully equip the hospital for the blind, to give shelter to the large number of unfortunates who lost their eyesight.

Well might the Governor-General thank President Wilson, as he did in the following message :

> "I desire to thank Your Excellency for your message, which the Canadian Government and I have received with profound appreciation and gratitude. We recognize in it and in the generous offers of assistance to the stricken city of Halifax, which have been received from many quarters of the United States, a further proof of that community of feeling which unites the two peoples in a bond of mutual sympathy and interest, so particularly appropriate at the present time, when both are engaged in a common purpose to vindicate the principles of liberty and justice, upon which the foundations of both governments rest."

A newspaper advertisement, seven weeks after the tragedy, which appeared on the day we landed, sounded an incongruous note of humour :

> "$25 Reward! Lost : a bull-dog. Not seen since the explosion."

Surely this is the hope which passeth understanding !

The Governor took us to lunch at the local club, where we met many prominent people of the town. We then walked a little in the city and visited some of the ruins, and so back to the ship.

And now comes the last stage of the journey. And if it were possible to describe these matters while the war continues, it would not be the least interesting.

But such things must wait. I may, however, say that where there is a danger zone I much prefer to take it at the beginning of the voyage than to reserve it for the end. In the former case, one is prepared for it at once, and the period is soon over. In the latter, the whole voyage seems a preparation for it. And such is the infirmity of human nature, and so limited the number of interesting topics on the sea, that everybody talks about the danger zone the whole time, until it is reached. Nor was anybody specially cheered by Mr. Baker's announcement, made two days before we sailed, that an intensive U-boat campaign may be expected in the near future, concentrated particularly in the Atlantic, so as to intercept the flow of

American troops to France, and American
food-stuffs to Allied countries. There were
large numbers of women aboard, and one or
two very small children. One was the age
of my little daughter, and was also called
Pamela. She became a friend.

The measures taken to defeat our enemy
are infinitely various, though obviously not
to be recorded. When we reach the actual
zone we are forbidden to move a yard without a life-belt. Many persons, resolved to be
found like the prudent virgins, with their
lamps burning, go to bed with all their clothes
on. Some, specially provident, have equipped
themselves with complete india-rubber suits,
almost like the kit of a diver. For these it is
claimed that they will support their wearer
in the water for days, and that they are indefinitely impervious to cold and water. This
I can believe, for surely there must be
some compensation in return for an appearance so completely ridiculous. Mr. George
McFadden, the senior partner of the greatest
cotton firm in the world, who has forsaken his
business to do war work in Paris, and is in my
boat, had one of these monstrous garments.
I very nearly persuaded him that it was necessary for him to appear during the daily boat

drill in his diving suit, but someone advised him in the contrary sense, and we therefore lost the happiness of this sight.

The weather continues to be extraordinary. We left Halifax in bitter cold. We shall probably find England in the ordinary weather of February. Yet for two days we have enjoyed delightful sunshine, and to-day (February 13th) I read for an hour on deck at 10.30 a.m. without a greatcoat. All day long the sun shone through the haze, and the little children played on deck. I have known it colder yachting in the Mediterranean in August. We are told the Gulf Stream is responsible. It is better to accept, without trying to understand, these mysteries. The sea is almost dead calm. No moon, but, otherwise, ideal weather for submarines.

I found on board Major Daly, Deputy M.F.H. of the Heythrop Hounds, under that fine old sportsman, Albert Brassey. I had last seen his square, scarlet back breaking away from Jolly's Gorse at the famous Bradwell Grove meet, and had tried to keep with him during the gallop to Williamstrip over the best wall country in England.

The ship is full of missions and their stenographers ; shipping missions, food missions, aeroplane missions. It is difficult to imagine a subject upon which one cannot get expert guidance, and much available information is here to check our American impressions. There is even a Japanese mission, consisting of nine men and a lady.

And everywhere, strong, vigorous young American soldiers, full of high spirits, but always good-natured and civil. You cannot sit in the smoke-room without hearing a worse French accent than you are accustomed to use yourself.

I greatly doubt whether the Mercantile Marine is receiving all the recognition from the Government to which it is entitled. It runs grave risks every hour of the day and night. It has only threatened to strike twice, and we remember the occasions. That some of its most distinguished officers take that view is undoubted. It would seem to me that all the experienced captains of all the great ships, which are to-day doing the King's work, and feeding the King's people, or conveying the troops of the King or his Allies, should be entitled to wear the King's uniform in the R.N.R. Let none suppose they do not wish to do so. We live in days when brave men are risking their lives everywhere, every day. No one does so more constantly and with a greater weight of overpowering responsibility than the Masters of the Mercantile Marine. It would be a very small thing to give them the right of wearing the King's uniform with honorary rank in the R.N.R. In their view, and here I speak with knowledge, it would be an indication to the world when they go ashore of the quality and value of their services.

I have myself met a young and very capable officer, who has been torpedoed twice, and has eight times volunteered for combatant service in the Navy. He was told (and I have no doubt truly) that his experience in the Mercantile Marine rendered him indispensable in that service. But a month later, in virtue of the fact that he had qualified himself by passing his gunnery course with great credit, he was given the honorary rank of Lieutenant in the R.N.R. He is a married man and, as may be supposed, not rich. But delighted with the right of wearing a uniform on shore which showed that he, too, was risking his life in the service of his country, and had the honour of bearing a combatant commission from His Majesty, he went to the expense of buying the whole uniform.

Recently he received a communication from their Lordships of the Admiralty, I think, to be fair, under a previous Administration, to the effect that a change of policy was in contemplation, and that, while he was thanked for his zeal and past services, it was not proposed to continue either his commission, or those of officers in a similar position.

As a memento, therefore, of a short career as a commissioned officer, he has the privilege of retaining the King's uniform, paid for by himself, which he is not allowed to wear. And this officer has in the first place combatant efficiency, and in the second place, is daily rendering, at the risk of his life, services absolutely essential to the life of the Nation. And he greatly resents his treatment.

I do not know what actual progress has been made in the scheme of giving decorations and service ribbons to the Mercantile Marine. But if it has not been done, it ought to be done at once. Everyone knows the nature of the services rendered by our sailors. Everyone knows how much these brave men

value the symbol of service faithfully rendered
to King and Country. Any regimental officer
in France will tell you the effect which this
form of recognition (and the hope of it) have
upon the morale of his men. Let the sailors
too enjoy the outward and visible signs of
their merit to sustain them while they are still
engaged in their dark and dangerous adven-
ture. Do not let them walk the streets of
our ports as if they had not rendered notable
service to their fellow countrymen.

The second steward in the dining-room
here, an elderly man, has twice found himself swimming for his life in stormy seas.
And he told me that in the room, as he spoke,
were ten men who had been torpedoed
oftener, and the dining saloon is full of
courteous, competent, grey-haired stewards,
who do their work with the most absolute
composure and civility, never knowing from
moment to moment when they may find
themselves plunged in the icy water of the
wintry Atlantic. But that one day or
another they will have this fate is almost
certain, if the war lasts long enough. And
what is to be said of the stokers ? Is any
class of man in any theatre of the war playing
a more dangerous, a nobler, or a more in-

dispensable part ? Surely, we take these things far too much as a matter of course. Every stoker nowadays is a hero, and the crazier and slower the engine he drives to sea, the greater the measure of his heroism. Tramp steamers, encouraged by no convoys, screened by no destroyers, and protected by no airships, have played no small part in securing (if it has been secured) the safety of Great Britain.

I am glad to end this book with a tribute to the Mercantile Marine of Great Britain, a breed worthy to spring from the stock which in one century ransacked with Drake the Spanish Main, and in another, fought, when kidnapped by the Press Gang, better than the seamen of any Navy in the world.

The days in the danger zone pass one by one. No meal is served to any passenger who forgets his life-belt. The ship's discipline is inexorably strict. We multiply entertainments to make the time go more quickly.

One day has its athletic sports, another a keenly-contested boxing contest. And each night the careless strains of a lively concert float over the ship from the drawing-room.

And so at last we catch, still safe, but not without an occasional alarm, the first glimpse of England, air-raided, rationed, war-worn and self-disparaging, but still how much the best and dearest country in the world! Let an Englishman be forgiven this reflection, as once again he sees the swarm of undaunted British destroyers collect for the protection of British ships and American soldiers.

Fabula jam narrata est.

To-morrow to the Prize Court.

APPENDIX No. I

On the Administration of the Military (or Selective) Service Law in the U.S.A.

By Harold Smith, M.P., Barrister-at-law.

In the month of May, 1917—one month after the declaration of war—the United States Government passed what is known as the Selective Service Law, which provided *inter alia* for the raising of Military forces by compulsion. As in England, at the outbreak of war, there was in the States no law operative which authorized any form of conscription. The Act of 1863, which authorized the compulsory raising of drafts for the civil war, had long since expired under the terms of its own limitations.

Nothing could more clearly illustrate the spirit of the country than the immediate decision to adopt compulsion. No part of its warlike preparations has been carried out so efficiently, so expeditiously or so smoothly.

It is well to remember that the vast machinery of registration had to be applied to a country of about three million square miles area, with a population of nearly 110 millions, of whom about 10 million men were under the military age of 31.

While the Bill was still in its early stages in

Congress, and within a few days of the outbreak of war, the first preparations were already on foot. The Governors of all States were being consulted by Washington, and their views and suggestions invited as to the best means of smoothly giving effect to the decision of the Government to compile a register of the whole people.

It is, moreover, a fact that practically the entire machinery was cut and dried before the law was passed on May 18th, 1917, all the Registration Boards had been appointed, and all their duties had been tentatively prescribed and defined. Even their necessary supplies had been forwarded, and, in fact, so elaborate and so exhaustive were the arrangements made in advance, that on the day the Law was passed the Provost Marshal General in Washington, the Directing Head, set the whole machinery immediately in motion by telegrams to the Governors of all States.

This surely constitutes a remarkable example of zeal and organizing ability, and it is the less surprising that, with such a start, the registration of these millions was carried out practically in one single day between definitely fixed hours.

But, even so, having regard to the size of the country, the difficulty and necessary delay in composing, harmonizing and, above all, distributing the prodigious amount of literature, regulations, instructions, registration cards, and all the numerous forms and various supplies necessarily associated with such a work, it must be accounted a marvellous performance that it was completed within twenty days after the Act was formally approved.

After registration there followed the even greater and more complex problem of determining liability for service, and establishing the elaborate machinery whereby effect could be given to the new law.

Ten million men of military years had registered, and all such men had now to be classified, and all had the right, under the law, to submit reasons to the statutory authority, if they desired to do so, in support of claims for exemption.

In considering the question of liability and exemption, it must be borne in mind that, of the ten million men of military years, it was not possible that the Military authorities could actually make use of more than about a million and a half for many months. On the other hand, a proportion of this ten million were aliens, and consequently relied upon as an asset under the Act, unless they had taken the steps preliminary to naturalization.

It is, for this reason, a little surprising to us at home, where the necessity for obtaining every man available is so great, to find that the American Act is, on the whole, a little more stringent than our own Military Service Acts in that the grounds for exemption do not appear to be quite as wide as our own.

It must be understood that every citizen of the United States of America, between the age of 21 years and 31 years inclusive, is *ipso facto* liable to and included in the Draft, provided he is not pronounced medically unfit.

A man may be discharged from the Draft if he satisfies the statutory authority :

1. That he has persons who are dependent on the salary or the wages which he earns. This is strictly construed, and any private means of husband, wife or dependents which provides for a modest and reasonable living, excludes any claim.

2. That at the date of the Act he was, in fact, a member of a religious sect, one of the tenets of which is an objection to fighting or taking life. This again is strictly construed, and no individual not a member of such a sect has any claim to exemption, and no one has any exemption granted except from combatant service—I understand that there are in all about ten or fifteen of these sects (some of them very obscure) and that there is practically no rooted objection to service, but only to combatant service. Whether this is so or not, the gratifying fact remains that only in the rarest cases do claimants, however much opposed to combatant service, decline non-combatant service.

3. That his occupation is such as to entitle him to exemption. This claim may be divided under any of three heads.

(a) That his work is necessary to the State. I understand that the construction placed upon this claim was in the early days so narrow as to render it practically impossible to obtain exemption unless the claimant could establish that the State would be directly injured if he were taken from his civilian occupation, and that consequently farm hands and even farmers failed to establish so bold a claim.   A more generous, and, if I may say so, a more common-sense view, is now taken, and a claim under this head would appear, as at home, to resolve itself into a question as to whether it is desirable in the National interest (having regard to the requirements of the Military) that the man should remain in civilian employment.

(b) That he follows an occupation which the President has certified as a war industry. As a rule, the employer proves that his industry is a certified one and that the man's services are essential.   In such a case, it is unusual for the Board to refuse a certificate of exemption.

(c) That he belongs to a class which has been certified as absolutely exempt under the Act.   This class includes :

    Members of Congress,

    Heads of Departments at Washington,

    Clerical Staffs in Government Departments,

    State Officials,

    The Judiciary,

    The Clergy of all denominations.

I have said that, as compared with our own Acts, the " Selective Service Law " is, on the whole, more stringent. In support of this view, I would draw attention to the fact that in the latter, there is no statutory exemption on the ground of personal hardship (except in the case of dependents absolutely dependent on the man's wages). We are all familiar at home with the most poignant cases of hardship, often entailing, were a man to be called up, the throwing away of a life's work at the age of perhaps forty or forty-one. All such a man's savings may be sunk in his business, and the sacrifice which he is called upon to make has been recognized by the State, though such are the exigencies of the Military situation that Tribunals often have recently felt themselves compelled to call upon very many British subjects to make even this great sacrifice.

No such pressure can be necessary in the States, having regard to their man power and geographical position, and yet, by their Statute, whatever the financial sacrifice, the man must serve if he or his dependents have an income which keeps them, not according to their rank of life, but according to reasonable requirements of persons entitled to live in modest comfort without luxury.

I have already pointed out the great advantage which the conscientious objector has under our Acts, and merely recall the fact now as another instance in which the Selective Service Law is more stringent.

It now remains to consider the statutory authorities which decide the claims, and which correspond to our Local and Appeal Tribunals. Of these, there are two—the one known as the Local Exemption Board, and the other as the District Appeal Board. There is an appeal, as of right, from the former to the latter.

The local Boards were appointed by the President, who invited the Governors of the States to recommend the personnel ; and, as a rule, the County Registration Boards, which quickly and efficiently carried out the work of the registration, were nominated *en bloc*. I might add, as a matter of interest, that a medical man was appointed to serve as a member of each such Board to advise on medical claims.

Some idea of the immense labour involved may be derived from the fact that, on the average, three men out of five made some sort of claim for exemption or discharge.

All claims for exemption on the ground of occupation are lodged with and determined by the District Appeal Board, and not the Local Board. The District Board, therefore, has a dual capacity in that it is the appeal authority from the Local authority, and also determines original applications on claims based upon occupation.

I must add that, in the great majority of cases, oral evidence was not submitted, and the applications and appeals were dealt with on documents alone. A somewhat curious provision allows (in exceptional cases only) a further appeal, as of right, to the President. I cannot cite authority for the view, but I believe that all such appeals are first considered and the necessary recommendations made by the War Department.

As in our Acts, the onus of proof is on the man. No one is entitled to exemption or discharge unless found physically unfit, or unless he has applied for exemption and satisfied the Board that he was entitled thereto. This has been so strictly construed that there are many cases where an alien has been called to the colours, and although on a motion for a writ of " habeas corpus " he has proved that he is an alien, the writ has not issued if through his own laches he has failed to lodge his claim on his appeal within the statutory time.

I do not know that this decision has, as yet, been confirmed by the Supreme Court. It will, perhaps, some time require consideration whether any country can, in the absence of an internal convention, enforce military service upon the subjects of another country.

It would not be right that I should leave this subject without paying a very high tribute to the army of voluntary workers who have been responsible for the immense task of registration, and for the administration of the Selective Service Law. It is estimated that nine-tenths of the work has been carried out without any expense to the Federal Government.

In every State and in every locality, men and

women in every station of life have volunteered their services in connection with registration, physical examination and clerical work ; without thought or desire for pay or reward.

Newspapers have, unrewarded, devoted unlimited space to make public all information submitted to them. They have even given in their columns the names of persons effected by any new regulations, or by successive steps taken in the Draft.

Lastly, the several State Governments have placed at the disposal of the Federal Government their entire machinery, their expert and general staffs, and have contributed everything in their power to assist in the administration of the Law.

It is difficult to conceive a greater manifestation of public spirit and general interest in the result, or a greater intensity of purpose than has been manifested throughout the administration of the most difficult and intricate problem. While the actual work to date has been confined to the great preliminary step of registration, and the turning of 687,000 men to the various branches of the Army, yet the ground work has been successfully and fully laid for the future needs of the military service, and it is believed that the remaining problems have been greatly simplified by the enormous amount of labour already performed.

APPENDIX No. II

On the Publicity Organization known as the " Division of Four-Minute Men "

By Harold Smith, M.P., Barrister-at-law.

In Great Britain we are now very familiar with the great campaigns organized from time to time by the Government, with the object of making direct and effective appeals to the people on matters of vital consequence arising out of the war.

These campaigns have centred round questions as varied and as fundamental as recruiting, war loans, national service and food economy. That they must continue there can be little doubt ; that they have entailed an almost prodigal expenditure of money and energy there can be less doubt. It may, therefore, be not unprofitable to consider a most effective and economical system of Government advertising adopted by the Committee on Public Information in a country which we at home have always believed, has not a great deal to learn in the subtle and necessary arts of advertisement. We may usefully ask ourselves whether the scheme, of which I give some details below, might not be developed in our own country as an effective, and, above all, an economical means of access to the great mass of the people, who do not attend meetings, or do not read wall posters and newspaper advertisements.

The month that the United States entered the war, President Wilson, by an Executive Order, created a Committee on Public Information, appointing thereon a civilian, Mr. George Creel, as Chairman, and the Secretary of State, the Secretary of War and the Secretary of the Navy.

As the name implies, it is the duty of this Committee to publish to the American nation, by any and every means in their power, all such news and information as, in the opinion of the Ministers, may encourage education and interest in war topics.

I do not propose to follow the many activities of this representative and efficient body, but to examine very shortly the work of a branch of this organization known as the " Division of Four-Minute Men," and formed by order of the Committee on Public Information, with the expressed approval of President Wilson.

The purpose of this body is thus shortly and officially set forth :

" The Four-Minute Men, a Nation-wide organization of volunteer speakers, was organized June 16th, 1917, for the purpose of assisting the various departments of the

Government in the work of National Defence during the continuance of the war, by presenting messages on subjects of vital National importance to motion-picture theatre audiences during the intermission. The subject matter is prepared, and the speaking is directed from Washington under the authority of the Government."

The organization is in charge of a Director, Mr. William McCormick Blair, appointed by the Committee on Public Information. In each State there is a Chairman, and in each city and community where the work is organized, there is a local Chairman, who enrolls a sufficient number of volunteer speakers to cover the motion-picture theatres in his city or community.

All officials and speakers are governed by "standardized" instructions and bulletins issued from Washington. These bulletins are very carefully prepared for each campaign, and are written either by the Editorial Staff in Washington, or by men of ability associated with the organization, and particularly qualified to deal with whatever is the subject of the campaign. The various chairmen now number about 3,400, and the total number of speakers is now over 20,000. All these are volunteers, and all submit to strict rules, the most strict (and perhaps to some the most irksome) being that under no circumstances must any speech extend beyond four minutes in time. However eloquent the "talk," however attractive the "talker," however interested the audience, and however difficult to find the peroration, the order must be obeyed, or (to quote from the official rules) the speaker "should be relieved of his assignment."

It is, perhaps, unnecessary to add that this great organization is only rendered possible by the co-operation and, indeed, the enthusiasm of the proprietors of the many thousand motion-picture theatres in the country, who readily offer the necessary facilities for four-minute speakers, and who undertake that no speeches shall be delivered in their theatres other than those under the auspices of the Committee on Public Information.

The subject matter of the speeches, as I have stated above, is taken from bulletins issued in Washington prior to the launching of each campaign. Some of the more important subjects dealt with in these campaigns are as follows :

The Two Liberty Loans,
The Red Cross,
Unmasking German Propaganda,
Food Conservation,
War Savings Stamps.

It will probably be admitted by those versed in these matters that, by this means of access to theatre audiences all over the country, Government messages may be attractively and directly delivered to the most democratic and to the largest audiences in the country, and, moreover, to audiences which represent all types of people and all shades of

opinion.   It most certainly has the advantage (not,
I think, hitherto associated with our own publicity
campaigns) that the work entails very little cost
to the State, in that the great army of men who
carry it on are volunteers.

The views of President Wilson on the work of
the organization are clear, and expressed in a
message to the workers which is inspiring and
encouraging.   I extract the following :

> " Men and nations are at their worst or at
> their best in any great struggle.   The spoken
> word may light the fires of passion and
> unreason, or it may inspire to highest action
> and noblest sacrifice a nation of free men.
> Upon you Four-Minute Men, who are charged
> with a special duty and enjoy a special
> privilege in the command of your audiences,
> will rest in a considerable degree the task of
> arousing and informing the great body of
> our people, so that, when the record of these
> days is complete, we shall read, page for page
> with the deeds of Army and Navy, the story
> of the unity, the spirit of sacrifice, the un-
> ceasing labours, the high courage of the men
> and women at home who hold unbroken the
> inner lines."

It is because the warring nations are more and
more realizing the value of publicity, and the
necessity of maintaining the morale of the nation,

that I have been invited to add this memorandum. I do so hoping that it may be of some slight interest and in the belief that a nation is thrice armed which clearly knows the justice of its cause, the value of what it defends and the justification for the sacrifices it is called upon to make.

APPENDIX No. III

THE AMERICAN PRESS IN WAR

I was always very careful to read the principal American papers in all the towns we visited. It is naturally interesting to observe under the stress of war the demeanour of a Press which has always claimed great licence. There are many points of resemblance between newspaper tradition in Great Britain and the United States. The Press of both countries has for generations been absolutely free. Neither has learnt to submit to any trammels, except such as are imposed by the Law of Libel. And this deterrent is far less formidable in the United States, where large pecuniary damages are practically never given in actions of defamation, than in England.

But a war like the present cannot tolerate complete freedom of newspaper publication. We had this problem to determine in England in August, 1914. We solved it by the creation of a Press Bureau. Nothing of the kind had ever been known in England. Everybody resented both its creation and its control. It was the target of universal criticism. I had the misfortune to be its first Director and organizer, being followed in this invidious task by the late Lord Chancellor, Lord Buckmaster. He would not, I think, dispute the statement that the system, for good or bad, which I organized in the first seven weeks of the war, has in its main features survived three and a half years' experience, and still supplies the methods by which the Press in this country is controlled. And this, at least, is a claim which none would be ambitious to dispute with me.

Our methods of censorship had been greatly criticized in the United States. It seemed to me that many of the censures passed upon us in the early days of the war ignored alike its gravity, and the novelty and complexity of the duties which we had undertaken. There was, indeed, as far as I could judge, a general feeling in the United States that all their news and all their cables should be allowed to proceed exactly as if no war had been in progress. I had many interviews with American journalists and men of business in the early days of the war, and I tried, and sometimes succeeded, in making them realize our difficulties. Nor do I think that I always failed, where circumstances allowed, to give them substantial concessions. This was certainly true of the cable delays, which caused so much complaint.

There were many people in England who thought that the whole system of a coercive Press censorship was wrong. They claimed, and with a great deal of justice, that no appeal had ever been made

in vain to the honour and patriotism of the Press
of Great Britain.   And they argued that a system
in which the Press was, so to speak, put upon its
honour, was preferable to one in which it was
threatened with the iron hand.   There was much
to be said for this contention, but I myself was
unable, on the whole, to agree with it.   There
were some papers, though not many, which could
not be trusted.   And it was necessary that authority should not be powerless where the appeal
to loyalty failed.   And so the Press Bureau was
established.   And then followed eight weeks of
the hardest, the most anxious and the most thank-
less work which my life has known.   We never
worked in that harassing period less than fifteen
hours a day.

In the United States, the Administration has
decided to rely mainly upon the loyalty of the
newspapers.   I say " mainly " because the ordinary
American law is strong enough to deal with cases
which amount to " aiding " the enemy.   It may
well be that their experience will prove that the
course I recommended in England was wrong.   But
the war has by no means proceeded for a sufficiently
long period in the United States to justify a definite
conclusion at this stage.   Nearly all the newspapers
observe, with the greatest possible public spirit
and loyalty, the indicated wishes of the Administration.   But they complain almost as loudly of
the limitations imposed upon them by these views
as our Press complained in the early days of the

war. While there is much discontent, and very much criticism, I hardly detected a case in which an important paper did not attempt to conform to the views of the Government. In one respect—but this, on a fundamental point—the British and American Governments, as might be expected from their traditions, have adopted the same view. No paper is in any way prevented from criticizing, and even from attacking the Government, if it thinks proper to do so. And, indeed, the attacks upon Mr. Baker reminded me very much of the campaign formerly conducted by an influential section of the British Press against Mr. Asquith. In other words, no attempt has been made in the United States to prevent political criticism, even of the severest character, against the Administration. But I seldom saw criticisms which did not seem to me to be intended helpfully. And it is, of course, indisputable that the editors of almost all the important papers are patriotic citizens, who are trying all the time to mould public opinion in such a manner as to help and not impede the war. I particularly wish to make a further tribute. The imaginativeness of the American interviewer has become proverbial. The shortness of my stay rendered it desirable that I should give interviews in every town I visited immediately on my arrival. Altogether I gave forty-eight such interviews in the United States and Canada, all of which were published with prominence in the Press. It was not possible, in any case, that I should require a proof of the interview before it appeared. Yet, in only one case, in all those interviews, was I gravely misrepresented. Not once, with the above exception, had I to make a single correction. Having regard to the German and Irish elements, which are to be found in the American Press, this is a very remarkable circumstance. It is, therefore, a reasonable claim, that the whole of the American Press—that mighty instrument for the influencing of public opinion—is doing its best to help the President, and to win the war.

Were I to attempt a note of friendly criticism, I should say that, with the exception of three or four great daily papers, there was, perhaps, sometimes a failure to present the war day by day in its proper perspective in relation to local and ephemeral matters. After all, this is the greatest war in which the United States has ever been engaged. The honour of the Nation has been deeply pledged by the President (with its own full consent) to carrying it to a successful issue. The task is one of stupendous and ever-growing difficulty. I cannot help thinking that if the loyal editors of the United States were to meet together,* realizing the difficulty of the task to which their country is committed, and consider, putting their brains into the common stock, how they could best help, daily and nightly, in pressing these matters upon their countrymen,

* As our editors in England have done since the war began. But I make this suggestion with anxiety, for perhaps they are already meeting !

they could render service of incalculable value to the allied cause. They are very able and experienced men, and they thoroughly understand the public for which they write.

There are, of course, many papers which before America came into the war were frankly pro-German. Some of these were undoubtedly the recipients of Bernstorff's disinterested generosity. Others, quite honestly, and at that time, from their point of view, quite legitimately, wrote to please their German readers. It must not be forgotten in this connection that an extraordinary number of papers appears in America in the German language. During my visit I had some of these translated out of curiosity. I did not discover a disloyal sentence in any one of them. Prudence, no doubt, counsels reticence, but there was some positive evidence of good feeling.

The case of the Hearst newspapers is, of course, altogether different. The management of these papers has always been (and I have no reason to doubt, from conviction) bitterly anti-English. Their proprietor owns about seventeen newspapers and magazines, and controls the policy of papers in Boston, New York, Atlanta, Chicago, San Francisco and Los Angeles. His leading organ in New York has, it is believed, a daily circulation of 450,000 copies. He himself is understood to claim for all his papers a daily audience of five million people.

Before America came into the war nothing in the view of Mr. Hearst which the Germans did was wrong, and nothing which the Allies did was right, and he or his editors wrote with so much force, and apparent conviction, that no foreigner is entitled to question his or their sincerity. Even after the sinking of the *Lusitania*, one of his organs invited the American public to sympathize " with poor, bleeding, suffering Germany." And after the American Government had declared war upon Germany, Mr. Hearst demanded in a signed letter an immediate peace rather than send " a million of our splendid young Americans every year to be offered up to the bloody sacrifice of war."

I have no right, and certainly no desire, to question the complete honesty of Mr. Hearst's conviction. And no one can dispute his absolute right, in the old days, to urge his views of a great crisis upon his fellow countrymen. He did so with great perseverance and great ability. The excesses of German policy defeated in the old days of neutrality his legitimate purpose. To-day his country is at war. Its honour and its security are alike involved. The choice has been irrevocably made. Few American citizens have a greater stake in the reputation and the safety of the United States than Mr. Hearst. His energy and enterprise are known to all the world. Members of his family (so I am told) are doing distinguished war work ; and I for one shall be surprised if this remarkable man does not throw his matchless influence into the only path which marches with the honour of America.

It is right to close this brief examination of the

attitude of the American Press, as a whole, by an expression of warm admiration for the ability and patriotism which inspire the overwhelming majority of American newspapers. Their liveliness, or, as it is called there, " snappiness " has long been the wonder of the world. It is reinforced to-day by the qualities of gravity and responsibility.

APPENDIX NO. IV

THERE has been so much disparagement in England of the extent and value of our military efforts; there has been so great a tendency to belittle our powers of organization—that I think it worth while allowing the military expert of the *New York Times*, an extremely competent critic, to put forward some considerations in the opposite sense. This gentleman writes with an authority which would be increased and not diminished if his identity were revealed. He contributed the following article to the issue of the *New York Times*, dated January the 27th, of the present year:

MILITARY CRITIC'S REVIEW

COMPARATIVE RECORD OF ENGLAND AND UNITED STATES IN PREPARING TO FIGHT

BY A MILITARY EXPERT.

On the 31st of January, 1917, Germany sent to us her message of an unrestricted submarine warfare, with her permission to send ships to Falmouth once a week. It was practically a declaration of war, and was so considered. Three days later Count von Bernstorff received his passports, and from that day war was inevitable. Bernstorff himself had warned us that, if we sent him home, war would follow. Therefore, we do not go very far astray when we say that war with Germany had practically existed since February 3rd, 1917. If this is not strictly true, as an historical fact, as a military fact it is true, because it is doubtful if there could be found among nations leaders so dense and so narrow-visioned as to fail to begin military preparations under such circumstances.

The country accepted war as inevitable. In fact, when it was formally declared in April there was not the slightest surprise or flurry. It was accepted as coming in the normal course of events. It is presumed that our military leaders looked at the situation in the same light, and, therefore, this review, when it speaks of the United States having been at war for a year, refers to the year which began on the 3rd of February last.

When one begins to consider this country at war for a year and begins to study what has been accomplished, there comes to mind the other English-speaking land—England—and we wonder how the two lands compare, due regard being had for the resources of the two in those things which go to make up a modern war machine. The purpose of this review is to compare or contrast the accomplishments of the two countries. England will, for the present purpose, be considered aside from her colonies, so that all figures and statements refer to the United Kingdom alone—that is, to the British Isles.

The total standing army of Great Britain when she declared war on Germany consisted of 425,000 men, scattered throughout the world in the thousand-and-one places where the British colonies lie. At home, in the United Kingdom, there were but about 100,000 men.   There were also in the United Kingdom about 100,000 militia, similar to our National Guard, although probably somewhat better trained and equipped.

In the United States the situation was somewhat similar.   Our regular army was about the same size as that which Great Britain had at home, and our National Guard, although possessing a paper strength of much greater proportions, had, in actual numbers, about another 100,000.   Many of the latter had had active, or semi-active, service on the Mexican border, which, to some extent at least, fitted them for field service.   But in one respect we had a distinct superiority—in the question of prospective officers.   The so-called business men's camps, which were afterwards turned into the Reserve Officers' Camps, had given us a number of men, most of them suitable officer material, who, with little additional training, would serve as the nucleus for the officers of a really large army.

Great Britain had nothing of this sort. In the early days of the war the most desperate need was for officers. The proportion of casualties among the officers was unusually great and placed an appalling drain upon such sources as England possessed. This was further complicated by the always unfortunate and undemocratic volunteer system which prevailed until February, 1916. Under this system many of England's best men, men who were ideal officer material, found their way into the rank and file of the army, and served as privates.

The advantage at the outset, then, if there was an advantage, lay with us. In numbers the men were practically the same, while in officers we were a long way ahead.

THE RACIAL PROBLEM

The British Isles, however, possessed a population of but 45,000,000, while that of the United States is about 110,000,000. There is, of course, a vast difference in the populations of the two countries. There is nothing racial in ours ; consequently no race pride, traditions, ties, or standards. In fact, there are as many different standards as there are elements in our population. The result is that there is great difficulty in finding any one appeal which will draw together, behind a given movement, all of the many elements of our population. There is, again, the fact that many of our inhabitants are not citizens, and that many of our naturalized citizens are of German birth or extraction. Of the latter, of course, the great majority are regarded as being loyal, although the acts of aggression of a few have been calculated to bring suspicion on the loyal majority. In England this problem did not exist to anything like the same extent. With the exception of the south of Ireland, England has had nothing to fear at home. The Germans in England have been easily taken care of, a task made simple by the relatively small area of the country. There is, in addition, the strong racial tie which binds the population together, the pride of race.

In other ways, however, our position was much more favourable. We possessed all of the raw material needed for war purposes. The United States is by far the greatest producer of both steel and coal. Great Britain has had to import the greater part of both of these products over a line of communication three thousand miles long. The same is true of nearly all of the other raw materials which enter into war manufacture. The question of food is equally vital. Great Britain is not self-supporting, cannot be under any conceivable conditions. She must import practically all of the foodstuffs which she consumes. We, on the other hand, are completely independent of the rest of the world for our necessities, except in the matter of sugar.

Of the conditions in which war found the industrial systems of the two countries there is no comparison at all, but a strong contrast. The war caught England utterly unprepared, not alone in man power, but in manufacture as well. It is hardly too much to say that there was not a plant in England with any material output devoted to or equipped for the manufacture of guns, rifles, or the munitions of war. There was no reason why there should have been. While the life of England is her carrying trade, both import and export, the English have never devoted themselves to any extent to the exportation of war materials. We, on the other hand, had been making war materials for the Allies for two and a half years. There was hardly a factory in the United States which, at the time we declared war, was not making war supplies for the Allies. And there was scarcely a type of war supply which was not at some point in the United States being manufactured for the war in Europe. In a practical sense, then, our industries were well prepared for war, ready to produce war materials on a large scale—in a large measure they were mobilized for war. All that was necessary was to place them under government control.

This gives what seems to be a fair estimate of the relative situation of the two countries at the time each entered the great conflict. We may, therefore, turn to what has been accomplished in each.

ENGLAND'S FIRST STEPS

The first step Great Britain took was to throw

into France her regular army of 100,000 men. This was, as a matter of fact, all she had agreed to do on land under her contract with the French. With this army was sent also its complement of artillery as it existed at that time. England's first contingent was practically wiped out in the retreat from Mons and the subsequent fighting on the Marne and the Aisne, but was reinforced by recruits hurriedly raised, so that it had been augmented by April 30th, 1915, by about 300,000 men. In the meantime England had become engaged in other quarters. A protectorate had been declared over Egypt, and about 60,000 men had been sent there to protect the eastern approach to the Suez Canal, where the Turks had shown signs of attack. The landing on Gallipoli had also been made and about 100,000 were engaged there. These, however, were mostly Australians and New Zealanders—Anzacs, but they were in great measure supplied and fed from England, so that not all of the burden was taken from Great Britain by the man power sent by her colonies. Moreover, although the Canadians began to arrive in December, 1914, their artillery was not brought overseas, but was supplied by the United Kingdom.

In February, 1915, the British were sufficiently strong to launch the attack at St. Eloi and follow it up a short time later with the battle of Neuve Chapelle. Early in May, Kitchener's first hundred thousand went into the trenches. From that time to the end of the first year there was a constant influx of men from England to the Continent, although no figures are available for the number of men England actually had in the trenches on August 1st, 1915, a year after she entered the war.

There had been manufactured, however, a great supply of artillery of all calibres, and the production of shells had grown to 50,000 per day. This gave the English sufficient reserve to launch the terrific attack at Loos in September, 1915, and to precede it by what was up to that time the heaviest bombardment of the war. Most of the material in this bombardment was made in England, although the raw stock was exported from the United States. Without any figures as to the total number of men the British had thrown into the field by the end of October, 1915 (these figures have never been given out by the British War Office), the British casualty lists had mounted by that time to nearly 500,000 men.

AMERICA'S ACCOMPLISHMENT

As to what the United States has accomplished, we have fairly full data from the Senate's investigation, which has been in progress for some time. We have provided for a force of approximately 1,400,000 men, of whom about 1,200,000 have been placed in training. Against this, Great Britain had enlisted 2,000,000 volunteers in the same period. We have not yet furnished this force with its equipment in clothing or in rifles, although it is probable that this defect will be remedied in a short time now. We have let contracts for a great number of guns and of shells, and our arsenals are also busy manufacturing. We have as yet received no deliveries of moment, and there is no prospect of our own army in France being supplied from this side of the water until early summer. We have no machine-guns except for air-craft, for which purpose we have adopted the Lewis gun, which we were well prepared to turn out in large numbers, as a result of having executed large contracts for England. There is no possibility of getting the required supply of these until August. Considering, then, the entire equipment in all of its elements, it is perfectly true to state that there is not yet in Europe one complete American regiment fully equipped by the American government. As to the number of men we have in Europe, it is not permitted to speculate, but we can refer again to the published estimate of the War Department that we might expect to send 400,000 over by the early part of March, and we can, therefore, be assured that we have not a force of this size in Europe as yet.

While on the subject of our force in Europe, it is somewhat difficult to follow the mind of the censor, which refuses to disclose the front on which the American forces are held. The duty of the censor and the object of censorship would seem to be to conceal all news that might be turned to the advantage of the enemy. The Germans know and have known just where the American troops are. And yet our censor conceals the fact, as if he were hiding some great secret. To stimulate interest in the war we must have news of the war. And the more accurate the news, the more we believe in its accuracy, the greater the interest is going to be. The present idea of censorship seems to be to conceal all facts in connection with our part in the war which have any interest, whether that interest is from its nature confined to ourselves alone, or whether it would be of interest to Germany. It apparently makes little difference whether Germany is already fully aware of these facts or not. It is a fallacy which may have grave consequences, and might well be rectified before we become too deeply involved.

APPENDIX NO. V

POLITICAL PARTIES IN THE UNITED STATES

From notes kindly supplied by Professor Thomas
F. Moran, of Purdue University.

THE exact date of the origin of political parties in
the United States cannot be determined. Like many
other organizations, they were matters of growth,
and their development was a gradual process.

There were no real political parties in the United
States, based upon purely American issues, until
the time of the formation of the present Constitution. During the Colonial period, there were
groups or factions of men, calling themselves
Whigs and Tories, and sympathizing, in general,
with the members of the corresponding English
parties. When the break with the Mother Country
took place, the Whigs supported the Revolution,
and were sometimes called *Patriots*, while the Tories
opposed the movement for independence and were
called *Loyalists*.

The first real parties in the United States, based
upon American issues were the Federalist and the
Anti-Federalist. These grew out of the formation
and adoption of the Constitution. The Federalists

favoured a comparatively strong central Government, and advocated the adoption of the Constitution of 1787. The Anti-Federalists, on the other hand, being opposed to centralization and in favour of States Rights, attempted to prevent the ratification of the Constitution. Not being able to accomplish their purpose, they went out of existence at the opening of the national period, leaving the Federalists in control of the Government.

Party lines were not drawn in Washington's first administration, but such an alignment took place in the second, and developed very rapidly after it became known that Washington would not accept a third term. The parties resulting from this separation were the Federalist and the Democratic-Republican. The former, composed largely but not wholly of those who had favoured the adoption of the Constitution, now stood for a centralization of power and a liberal interpretation of the Constitution. The latter party insisted upon a strict or literal construction of the Constitution, and favoured States Rights. Alexander Hamilton and John Adams were leaders of the Federalists, while Thomas Jefferson was the recognized head of the Democratic-Republican party.

The Federalist party disappeared, owing to a variety of reasons, in the so-called "era of good feeling," in President's Monroe's time, and was succeeded, in a general way, by the National Republican party, under the leadership of John Quincy Adams and Henry Clay. This party was

18*

short-lived, and its lineal successor was the Whig Party, which succeeded in electing William Henry Harrison to the presidency in the famous campaign of 1840

The problems of slavery and the issues leading up to the Civil War split existing parties and caused a new alignment. In 1854, a group of parties and sections of parties, opposed to slavery, effected an amalgamation and formed the Republican party of the present day. General John C. Fremont was the first presidential candidate of the new party, and Abraham Lincoln its first successful candidate.

The Democratic-Republican party, founded by Thomas Jefferson in Washington's time, has continued in existence to the present day. In President Jackson's time the name was changed to Democratic, and has so continued.

The two great parties, then, in American politics at the present time, and since the Civil War, are the Republican and the Democratic. Minor parties of considerable strength and importance, such as the Prohibition, the Greenback, the Socialist, and the Populist, have existed for longer or shorter periods, and some of them are in existence at the present day. In the main, however, the Republican and Democratic are, and have been in recent years, the dominating parties in American politics.

A word of caution should, perhaps, be inserted at this point in regard to the succession of parties. When it is said that a certain party is the lineal successor of another, the statement should not be construed too literally. It is not true, for instance, that all of the Whigs, or even all of the Northern Whigs, became members of the new Republican party in 1854. Neither is it true that any particular party maintained its fundamental principles intact for any considerable number of years. Many modifications were made imperative by the practical exigencies of the times.

Mention should also be made at this time of the movement which caused a split in the Republican party in 1912. A few years prior to that date, some of the progressive members became restless under the more conservative policies of the men in control of the party. The result was the so-called " insurgency " movement. The " Insurgents " became the nucleus of the Progressive party, which was launched in Chicago in the summer of 1912. In the Republican National Convention of that year, Theodore Roosevelt was the candidate of the Progressive element of the party for the presidential nomination, while the " old line " members supported President William Howard Taft. President Taft was nominated, and the Progressives, displeased with the methods and decisions of the National Committee, and of the nominating Conventions, withdrew and nominated Mr. Roosevelt as the candidate of the new Progressive party. The launching of this new party split the Republican vote into two parts, and Woodrow Wilson, the Democratic candidate was

elected to the presidency by a large majority of
the Electoral College. In 1916, however, the
breach was healed to a large extent. The Progressives made no nomination for the presidency,
and most of them supported Justice Charles Evans
Hughes, the regular Republican nominee. Mr.
Wilson, having been again nominated by the Democrats, defeated Justice Hughes in a close election.

The above constitutes a very brief and imperfect
sketch of the history of the political parties in the
United States. To state, within brief compass,
the fundamental principles of the two leading
political parties is not so easy. Historically, the
Republican is the Nationalist party, while the
Democratic is the party of States Rights. Historically, also, the Republican is the party of implied
powers, while the Democratic is the party of strict
construction. Fortunately, however, neither party
has been entirely consistent in its devotion to early
ideals. Each party has felt obliged at times by
the exigencies of affairs to set aside its theories in
the interest of practical results. The one issue,
however, which in recent years has divided the
two parties has been the tariff question. The
Republicans, in the main, have stood for a pro-
tective and very considerable tariff on imports,
while the Democrats have favoured a low tariff,
primarily for revenue. Just at the present
moment party lines are not being drawn. The
war has relegated purely partisan matters into
the background. The two parties are united

for the winning of the contest. All of the great war measures advocated by the President have been passed without regard to party lines. A Coalition Cabinet, somewhat similar to the one set up in England, has been advocated from time to time, but no such action has as yet been taken. The American political system does not lend itself as readily to a Cabinet of this kind as does the British.

Table I. shows, in a very general way, the succession of political parties in the United States, and Table II. shows the political complexion of the 65th Congress, which assembled in December, 1917.

TABLE I

Whig	Federalist	Federalist	National Re-publican	Whig	Republican
Tory	Anti-Federalist	Democratic-Republican		Democratic	

TABLE II

SENATE		HOUSE	
Democrats	52	Democrats	214
Republicans............	42	Republicans	212
Republican and Progres-		Progressive	1
sive	1	Independents	2
Vacancy	1	Socialist	1
		Prohibitionist	1
		Progressive-Protectionist.	1
		Progressive-Democrat ...	1
		Non-partisan	1
		Vacancy	1
Total	96	Total..............	435

INDEX

Printed at The Chapel River Press, Kingston, Surrey.

Foreign Travelers in America 1810–1935

AN ARNO PRESS COLLECTION

Archer, William. **America To-Day**: Observations and Reflections. 1899.

Belloc, Hilaire. **The Contrast.** 1924.

[Boardman, James]. **America, and the Americans.** By a Citizen of the World. 1833.

Bose, Sudhindra. **Fifteen Years in America.** 1920.

Bretherton, C. H. **Midas, Or, The United States and the Future.** 1926.

Bridge, James Howard (Harold Brydges). **Uncle Sam at Home.** 1888.

Brown, Elijah (Alan Raleigh). **The Real America.** 1913.

Combe, George. **Notes on the United States Of North America During a Phrenological Visit in 1838-9-40.** 1841. 2 volumes in one.

D'Estournelles de Constant, Paul H. B. **America and Her Problems.** 1915.

Duhamel, Georges. **America the Menace**: Scenes from the Life of the Future. Translated by Charles Miner Thompson. 1931.

Feiler, Arthur. **America Seen Through German Eyes.** Translated by Margaret Leland Goldsmith. 1928.

Fidler, Isaac. **Observations on Professions, Literature, Manners, and Emigration, in the United States and Canada, Made During a Residence There in 1832.** 1833.

Fitzgerald, William G. (Ignatius Phayre). **Can America Last?** A Survey of the Emigrant Empire from the Wilderness to World-Power Together With Its Claim to "Sovereignty" in the Western Hemisphere from Pole to Pole. 1933.

Gibbs, Philip. **People of Destiny**: Americans As I Saw Them at Home and Abroad. 1920.

Graham, Stephen. **With Poor Immigrants to America.** 1914.

Griffin, Lepel Henry. **The Great Republic.** 1884.

Hall, Basil. **Travels in North America in the Years 1827 and 1828.** 1829. 3 volumes in one.

Hannay, James Owen (George A. Birmingham). **From Dublin to Chicago**: Some Notes on a Tour in America. 1914.

Hardy, Mary (McDowell) Duffus. **Through Cities and Prairie Lands:** Sketches of an American Tour. 1881.

Holmes, Isaac. **An Account of the United States of America,** Derived from Actual Observation, During a Residence of Four Years in That Républic, Including Original Communications. [1823].

Ilf, Ilya and Eugene Petrov. **Little Golden America:** Two Famous Soviet Humorists Survey These United States. Translated by Charles Malamuth. 1937.

Kerr, Lennox. **Back Door Guest.** 1930.

Kipling, Rudyard. **American Notes.** 1899.

Leng, John. **America in 1876:** Pencillings During a Tour in the Centennial Year, With a Chapter on the Aspects of American Life. 1877.

Longworth, Maria Theresa (Yelverton). **Teresina in America.** 1875. 2 volumes in one.

Low, A[lfred] Maurice. **America at Home.** [1908].

Marshall, W[alter] G[ore]. **Through America:** Or, Nine Months in the United States. 1881.

Mitchell, Ronald Elwy. **America:** A Practical Handbook. 1935.

Moehring, Eugene P. **Urban America and the Foreign Traveler, 1815-1855.** With Selected Documents on 19th-Century American Cities. 1974.

Muir, Ramsay. **America the Golden:** An Englishman's Notes and Comparisons. 1927.

Price, M[organ] Philips. **America After Sixty Years:** The Travel Diaries of Two Generations of Englishmen. 1936.

Sala, George Augustus. **America Revisited:** From the Bay of New York to the Gulf of Mexico and from Lake Michigan to the Pacific. 1883. 3rd edition. 2 volumes in one.

Saunders, William. **Through the Light Continent;** Or, the United States in 1877-8. 1879. 2nd edition.

Smith, Frederick [Edwin] (Lord Birkenhead). **My American Visit.** 1918.

Stuart, James. **Three Years in North America.** 1833. 2 volumes in one.

Teeling, William. **American Stew.** 1933.

Vivian, H. Hussey. **Notes of a Tour in America from August 7th to November 17th, 1877.** 1878.

Wagner, Charles. **My Impressions of America.** Translated by Mary Louise Hendee. 1906.

Wells, H. G. **The Future in America:** A Search After Realities. 1906.